EX LIBRIS

Going to the Mountain

Life Lessons from my Grandfather, Nelson Mandela

NDABA MANDELA

HUTCHINSON
LONDON

1 3 5 7 9 10 8 6 4 2

Hutchinson
20 Vauxhall Bridge Road
London SW1V 2SA

Hutchinson is part of the Penguin Random House group of companies whose
addresses can be found at global.penguinrandomhouse.com.

Penguin
Random House
UK

This book is a work of non-fiction based on the experiences and recollections of
the author.

First published in the USA by Random House in 2018
First published in the United Kingdom by Hutchinson in 2018

www.penguin.co.uk

A CIP catalogue record for this book is available from the British Library.

ISBN 9781786331557 (hardback)
ISBN 9781786331564 (trade paperback)

Printed and bound in Great Britain by Clays Ltd, Elcograf S.p.A

Every effort has been made to trace copyright holders and to
obtain their permission. The publisher apologises for any errors or
omissions and, if notified of any corrections, will make suitable
acknowledgement in future reprints or editions of this book.

Page 134: lines between Rafiki and Simba, *The Lion King*, 1994,
Walt Disney Pictures.

Penguin Random House is committed to a sustainable future
for our business, our readers and our planet. This book is made
from Forest Stewardship Council® certified paper.

Contents

CONTENTS

"The struggle against apartheid can be typified as the pitting of memory against forgetting...our determination to remember our ancestors, our stories, our values and our dreams."

—NELSON MANDELA

Prologue

One of the last known photographs of my grandfather, Nelson Mandela, was taken at his home in Johannesburg on a Saturday morning in 2013, just a few weeks before he died. In that photo, my three-year-old son Lewanika sits on the arm of the Old Man's easy chair, looking with great interest at his Baba. My grandfather smiles a crooked smile, holding Lewanika's small hand, the same way he held mine the first time I met him at Victor Verster

Prison when I was seven years old. I have to smile at the similarities I see in the two of them: a very specific hairline, the same shell-shaped ear, and the way their eyes crinkled at the corners when they laughed at each other.

On this particular Saturday morning, the Old Man was quieter than usual. He was ninety-five years old and had been fighting a lingering upper respiratory infection, but the strength of his spirit was still evident in the way he held himself, and the strength of his character was evident in the way he held Lewanika. My grandfather loved children. To the end of his days, if you put the Old Man in a room with a baby or a little kid, you might as well not exist. Suddenly this great man—this revolutionary leader, this president, this historic agent of change—became as silly and softhearted as any granddad. He had eyes only for those little ones.

When I was a kid and it was just my granddad and me at the long dining room table, he said to me more than once, "All those years in jail, I never heard the sound of children. That is the thing I missed the most."

One dining room table, no matter how long, could not possibly be inhabited by two people who were more different. He was born in rural South Africa in 1918. I was born in urban Soweto in 1982. He was a giant, a national treasure; I was one of a thousand scruffy kids kicking cans down the street. It would have been easy for anyone to ignore me, and plenty of people did, but it wasn't in Madiba's character to ignore any child, no matter how poor, scruffy, or seemingly insignificant. He spoke with great longing and regret about being absent while his own children and grandchildren were growing up. He'd been in prison all of my life and most of the life of my father, Makgatho Lewanika Mandela, the Old Man's second son by his first wife, Evelyn Ntoko Mase. His intention, I think, was to make up for that a little by taking me in and becoming, in all functional aspects, a father to me. As with most good intentions, there were downsides he didn't anticipate, but somehow my grand-dad and I crossed the valleys that separated us.

Madiba's children, grandchildren, and great-grandchildren brought out a deep sense of hope in him, but also a deep sense of responsibility and a fresh respect for ancient tradition. He looked at us and saw both past and future: his ancestors standing alongside his descen-dants. I never fully understood that until Lewanika came along, followed by his little sister Neema, but I think I started to understand as the Old Man passed from his eighties into his nineties, and the roles we played in each other's lives began to reverse. My grand-dad was my protector and caregiver when I was a child; now I was his. During his final years, he didn't want a lot of strangers fussing over him. He wanted my older brother and me to carry him up the stairs and preferred to have his wife, Graça, help him with personal needs. If he was leaving the house, he wanted me to arrange security. If he was sitting up in bed, he wanted me to bring him the most relevant newspapers. I was that guy.

He often said to me, "Ndaba, I'm thinking of going to the Eastern Cape to spend the rest of my days. Will you come with me?"

"Yes, Granddad, of course," I always answered.

"Good. Good."

He never did return to the place of his boyhood. Perhaps he and I could never accept the concept of "the rest of my days." I wanted to think about the remainder of his life in terms of years, so the final moment took me by brutal surprise.

Even as he approached his mid-nineties, he never lost a bit of his zest for life, but he was pretty frail those last few years, and that frustrated him. He occasionally got quite combative, yelling at the nurses and caregivers. He even punched one male nurse in the face, much to everyone's shock and dismay. It was like the old boxer inside him had suddenly had enough of all this nonsense and—*bam*—he let loose a surprisingly strong left uppercut before anyone realized what was happening.

"Get out of here!" he bellowed at the poor bloke. "My

grandson will take care of you if you don't get out of our house! Ndaba! Fetch that stick!"

"Granddad, Granddad, whoa, whoa, whoa." I always tried to get in there and calm him down, but sometimes there was no soothing him. That big, deep voice could still rattle the roof. It was startling for those who didn't spend a lot of time with him, and for me, it was a terrible reminder that the Old Man was seriously getting *old*. I didn't allow myself to think about where that was leading. It's not our way for the men in my family to be nostalgic or sentimental. For five generations before I was born into apartheid, members of my family withstood every form of struggle, oppression, and violence you can imagine. This sort of history tends to thicken a man's skin. We go forward. We don't flinch.

"Ndiyindoda!" we shout at a crucial moment in *Ukwaluka*, the ancient circumcision rite whereby a Xhosa boy comes of age. It means, *"I am a man!"* The declaration defines us from that moment forward. *Ukwaluka*—"going to the mountain"—is a celebration, but the *abakhwetha* (the initiates, usually in their late teens or early twenties) must survive a month of rigorous physical and emotional trials. My grandfather described *Ukwaluka* as "an act of bravery and stoicism." The moment after the *ingcibi*, the circumcision specialist, makes that critical stroke of the

blade, the initiate shouts, *"Ndiyindoda!"* and he'd better mean it. There is no anesthetic, so there can be no fear. Flinching or pulling away could cause disastrous consequences. An infection can be fatal. There is some controversy surrounding the practice; young men have died. For many generations, it was shrouded in mystery, because let's face it, if you knew all the details, would you want to do it?

I won't lie: I felt a certain amount of dread during my teen years, knowing that someday I would be the one going to the mountain. I would be given my circumcision name and claim my place in the world. I would be a man. It sounded like a lot of work, to be honest, and my grandfather let me know he expected nothing less than this from me, but he didn't just tell me, "Be a man!" During the years that I lived with him—and during the years that I didn't—he lived his life as an example I couldn't ignore. He showed me that no ritual could make a boy a man. *Ukwaluka* is the outward expression of an inner transformation that has already taken place, and for me, that transformation was by far the most difficult task.

How strange to find that, at the end of this great man's life, taking into account all that he gave and taught me, the greatest privileges were in the smallest moments. His hand on my head when I was lonely or afraid.

His somber eyes as he lectured me across the dinner table. His rolling laughter and theatrical way of telling stories—and he did love telling stories! Especially the African folktales he grew up with. He even made a children's book, *Nelson Mandela's Favorite African Folktales*, and in the Foreword, he wrote, "A story is a story; you may tell it as your imagination and your being and your environment dictate, and if your story grows wings and becomes the property of others, you may not hold it back." He expressed a sincere wish that the voice of the African storyteller should never die, and he recognized that in order for that to happen, the stories themselves must evolve and bend to the ear of each new listener.

That is the spirit in which I offer the stories in this book—my story about my life with my grandfather, along with some of the old Xhosa stories and sayings—and in doing so, I hope to share the greatest life lessons I learned from Madiba. As I grow older, I see all these events in a new light, so I understand why others who witnessed the same events might see them differently. Human memory is more changeable and mysterious than any of those old stories about magical beasts and talking spiders and rivers that flow with souls of their own, but inevitably a story reveals the storyteller's heart, so even those fantastical tales tell very real truth. As I sit down to this task, I'm humbled by the knowledge that people all over the world—including my own children—will read this book, and I'm reminded of the Kenyan prayer for the spirit of truth: *From the cowardice that dares not face new truth, from the laziness that is content with half-truth, from the arrogance that thinks it knows all truth, may the gods deliver me.*

The stories of the Xhosa run deep with themes that resonated for Madiba and still strike a chord in me: justice and injustice, hidden truths revealed and grave wrongs righted, amazing metamorphoses and mystical happenings. Master storyteller Nongenile Masithathu Zenani, a curator of Xhosa oral tradition, says the story-teller's power is in *ihlabathi kunye negama*—"the world and the word." My grandfather understood a man's power to change his own story and the power of that story to change the world.

When I was a child, my story—my small world—was defined by two things: poverty and apartheid. When I was eleven years old, I went to live with my grandfather, who helped me reclaim a different vision of the world and my place in it. My early childhood was sometimes terrifying. My teenage years were complicated. I struggled in school. I partied hard to drown out the noise of the crowd and the painful absence of my parents. Some of the choices I made broke my grandfather's heart, and some of the choices he made broke mine. But over the years, always, always, there was a bond of good faith between us. He saw a good man in me and refused to let up until I saw that man in the mirror. I saw a great man in him and worked hard to be more like him.

I believe Madiba's words have the power to change your world too, and by that I mean both the world around you and the world within you, the undiscovered universe that is your own possibility. I believe Madiba's wisdom, amplified and embodied by you and me, still holds the potential to reshape the world we share and the world our children will inherit.

1

Idolophu egqibeleleyo iyakusoloko imgama.

"The perfect city is always a long way off."

The first time I met my grandfather, I was seven and he was seventy-one, already an old man in my eyes, if not in the eyes of the world. I'd heard many stories about the Old Man, of course, but I was a child, so those stories were no more real or relatable to me than the old Xhosa folktales repeated by my great-aunts and great-uncles and other

elderly people around the neighborhood. The Story of
the Child with the Star on His Forehead. The Story of
the Tree That Could Not Be Grasped. The Story of Nelson Mandela and How He Was Imprisoned by White
Men. The Story of the Massacre at Sharpeville. Fables
and folktales drifted around in the dusty streets and
got mixed in with the news on a car radio. Parables and
proverbs slipped through the cracks in the Bible stories
in the Temple Hall. The Story of the Workers in the
Vineyard. The Story of Job and His Many Troubles.

My father grew up a hustler on the streets of Soweto,
and for better or worse, a hustler is always good with a
story. The Story of Where I Was Last Night. The Story
of How Rich I'll Be Someday. Grownups all around me,
each according to their own belief system, repeated
their stories over and over, blowing smoke, tipping
beers, shaking their heads. Talk, talk, talk. That's all
I heard when I was a child. I wasn't really listening. I
never felt those stories steal under my skin and soak into
my bones, but that's what they did.

I was a smart little boy with a quick mind and a big
imagination, but I had no real understanding that my
family was at the center of a global political firestorm. I
didn't know why I was always being moved from place
to place or why people would either take me in or shut
me out—either love me or hate me—because I am a

Mandela. I was vaguely aware that my dad's father was a very important man on the radio and TV, but I couldn't begin to know how important he would become in my own life or how important I already was to him.

I was told that he loved my father and me and all his children and grandchildren, but I had seen no evidence of that, and I certainly didn't understand that there were people who thought they could use Madiba's love for us to bloody his spirit and bring him low. They thought the weight of his love might break him in a way that hammering rocks in the heat of the South African sun could not. They were mistaken, but they kept trying. First they let a large group of family members visit for his seventy-first birthday in July 1989. That must have been like a drop of water on the tongue of a man who's been dying of thirst for twenty-seven years, but Madiba still refused to yield any political ground, so six months later, they allowed a holiday visit on New Year's Day 1990, just a few weeks after my seventh birthday.

My father invested no drama in the announcement. He simply said, "We're going to see your grandfather in jail." Until that moment, such a suggestion was like saying we were hopping in the car to go meet Michael Jackson or Jesus Christ. People on TV seemed to believe that my grandfather was a bit of both: celebrity and deity. This turn of events was quite unexpected, but in

African culture, children don't ask questions. My father
and grandmother said, "We're going." So we went.

No further explanation was offered or expected,
but I was burning with curiosity. What would jail be
like? Would Grandmother Evelyn lead us through the
iron bars and down a cement hallway to a razor-wired
yard? Would heavy iron doors clang shut behind us—
and would someone remember to come back and let us
out? Would we be surrounded by murderers and thugs?
Would my aunts beat them off with their enormous
purses?

I was ready to fight, if necessary, to defend my family and myself. I was good with a stick. My friends and
I had sharpened our stick-fighting skills through years
of pretend fights in the dirt streets and trampled yards.
I rather enjoyed daydreaming about a great battle in
which I would be a hero, and there was plenty of time
for daydreaming as we made the thirteen-hour drive
from Johannesburg to Victor Verster Prison in a caravan
of five mud-encrusted cars loaded with Mandela wives,
children, sisters, brothers, cousins, aunts, uncles, babies,
and old folks. So you can imagine, it was a pretty long
trip.

We drove for what seemed like an eternity, through
rolling hills and across expansive savannahs to the
Hawequas Mountains. We turned south from Paarl,

a little town full of Dutch Cape houses with scrolled
white facades. Sitting in the back seat, I rolled down
the window and inhaled the clean scent of wet grape
leaves and freshly tilled soil. For a thousand years before
the Dutch East India Company came to this region in
the 1650s, it was the land of the Khoikhoi people, who
herded cattle and had great wealth. Now vineyards
dominated the landscape, and the mountain called Tor-
toise by the Khoikhoi had been renamed Pearl by the
Dutch. The mountain knew nothing of this, of course,
and as a seven-year-old boy, I was equally oblivious. I
saw only the vineyards, verdant green and rigidly in
order, and I accepted without thinking twice that this
was as it should be. I never questioned it, because as an
African child, I was taught not to ask questions, but now,
as a man—as a Xhosa man—as an African father and
son and grandson, I do wonder: At what point do the
roots of a vineyard sink so deep that they become more
"indigenous" than five hundred generations of cattle?

This sort of question is my grandfather's voice in my
head, even though it's been a few years since his death
and many more years since I went to live with him in a
rapidly spinning world where we broke and rebuilt each
other's idea of what a man is. His voice still rumbles
through my bones, bumping into the old stories. It has
settled into the marrow, like sediment in a river. As I

get older, I hear his voice coming from my own throat. Everyone tells me I sound like him, and knowing that I do makes me weigh my words a little more carefully, particularly in a public setting.

At the prison entrance, there was a small guard shack with a swing arm gate behind a white angled arch. A bright green sign with yellow lettering said: VICTOR VERSTER CORRECTIONAL SERVICES. Beneath this was inscribed: *Ons dien met trots*. ("We serve with pride.") It's possible that my aunts exchanged glances at the irony of that, but if they did, I didn't notice. I was staring up at the towering rocky faces of the mountains. Grownups chatted with the guards who leaned from the window of the guard shack. Talk, talk, talk. The guards hustled the two dozen Mandelas out of the five cars and into a large white van. Packed tightly on the hard bench seats, we were rolling again, but we didn't go to the big prison building with its high walls and coiled razor wire. We turned down a long dirt road, little more than a worn set of parallel tire tracks that led to the far, far back corner of the prison complex.

The van pulled to a stop outside an arched garage door, and we all got out in front of an attractive salmon-colored bungalow shaded by fir and palm trees. My grandmother and great-aunts were dressed up as if they were going to church or a special social event, so they stood out like exotic birds, all bold prints and bright colors, against the pale pinkish walls. My father and the other men present wore dress shirts and ties, and before they approached the gate, they shook their carefully folded suit coats and put them on.

The house was surrounded by a decorative garden wall that was not even as tall as my father. Two armed guards stood outside a little wrought iron gate—like a pretty little garden gate, not the dramatically clanging iron doors I'd imagined—and they greeted us and waved us inside. And there was my grandfather. I barely glimpsed his broad smile before he was engulfed in a wave of affection. The women were crying as they rushed to throw their arms around him, crying, *"Tata! Tata!"* which means "father." The men maintained stiff chins and straight postures, each waiting his turn to embrace the Old Man firmly, to grasp his hand and squeeze his shoulder. No tears, no tears. Only those firm jaws and hardy handshakes.

The children, including my brother Mandla, my cousin Kweku, and me, hung back, not quite knowing what to expect. To us, the Old Man was a stranger, and he seemed to understand this, smiling at us over the heads of our parents and grandparents, patient but eager to get to us and greet each one of us individually. When it was my turn, he took my small hand in his huge, warm grip.

"What's your name?" he asked.

"Ndaba," I said.

"Yes! Ndaba! Good, good." He nodded enthusiastically, as if he recognized me. "And how old are you, Ndaba?"

"Seven."

"Good. Good. What grade are you in? Do you do well in school?"

I shrugged and looked at the floor.

"What do you want to be when you grow up?" he asked.

I had no answer for that question, being a child who'd been shuffled from here to there. I had seen very little beyond the poverty and obstacles that surrounded me in the inner city, and I didn't want to embarrass myself by saying something dumb like "stick fighter."

The Old Man set his big hand on top of my head and smiled.

"Ndaba. Good."

He shook my hand again, very formal, very proper, and went on to greet the next child in line. The moment, I'm sorry to tell you, was not at all momentous. Sitting here now, trying very hard to remember the feeling—his hand on my head, that gigantic handshake, the towering height of his pant leg, the smell of linen and coffee when he bent down to hear my shy answers to his questions—nope. I got nothing. All of that was lost on me then. I've read what my grandfather wrote about it in *Long Walk to Freedom*. He was always reluctant to write about personal family matters, but he describes the house at Victor Verster as "a cottage" that was "sparsely but comfortably furnished." That made me laugh out loud when I read it, because to me as a kid from Soweto, this place seemed like a mansion.

The overstuffed sofa and matching easy chairs were like rose-colored clouds. The impeccably clean bathroom was the same size as the bedroom I shared with my cousins. A white man whose job was to cook and keep house for my grandfather came and went from the kitchen, trotting out a parade of platters and bowls and baskets of dinner rolls. Out back, there was a pristine blue swimming pool that made my skin itch to dive in. The pool was flanked by potted plants and surrounded by the garden wall. My grandfather told me later that the garden wall was topped by razor wire, but I was either too short to see that or too busy playing on the impossibly green grass. I couldn't have been more impressed if we'd found the Old Man locked up in the Ritz Hotel. The next time somebody asked me, "What do you want to be when you grow up?" I said, "I want to be in jail!"

Of course, the prison I expected to see that day was Robben Island, the stark hellhole where my grandfather had spent a large part of his life. As anti-apartheid sentiment grew around the world, the powers that be had Madiba moved to the house at Victor Verster in an effort to separate him from his friends and drive a wedge between the members of the African National Congress. His political foes hoped to chip away at his resolve with the seductive comfort of this pleasant little home and the promise that he could see his family: the wife who'd been imprisoned and tortured, the children he hadn't seen since they were small, the grandchildren he'd never seen at all. But his foes underestimated him. For two years, he maintained his resolve and held his ground in round after round of bitter argument over the future of South Africa. It would be a long time before I fully understood that my cousins and I were lolling that day with our feet up on the chairs where my grandfather routinely sat with powerful heads of state, embroiled in political and ideological debates that would soon alter the course of history.

As the day wore on, the grownups gathered in the kitchen and dining room, as grownups tend to do, and the kids flopped down on the carpet in the living room and popped a video tape of *The NeverEnding Story* into the VCR. I vaguely remember the adult voices rising and falling through laughter and lively conversation with my grandfather's resonant bass at the center of it all, but we had no interest in their conversation.

To be totally honest, I have to admit that my memory of that first meeting with my grandfather is quite hazy. I know what he was like that day mainly because I spent thousands of other days with him as I grew up and he grew old. For the exact details, I have to rely on what I've seen more recently about the place that's now called Drakenstein Correctional Centre. The bright green and yellow sign is still there, but people only see it because they're visiting the statue of my grandfather as a free man, bronze fist held high, striding out of Victor Verster on February 11, 1990. In my mind, the particulars of that family visit are a collage of recollection, newspaper clippings, and conversations with my grandfather, grandmother, Mama Winnie, and other old folks who were there. But I do remember one thing very clearly: *The NeverEnding Story.*

I suppose a Xhosa storyteller might call it "The Story of the Boy Who Saved the World from Nothing." In it (for those of you who have not seen this movie or read the book by Michael Ende), a boy goes on a perilous journey to overcome an invisible menace, The Nothing, which is slowly, steadily swallowing everything and everyone in the world. The daunting challenge facing the boy is that he must find a way to stop this invisible menace, but first, he must convince others that it exists. He must somehow win them over to the understanding that all those who have vanished had value and that the world now perceived as "normal" is not the world as it should be—and that the world *must change* in order to survive.

In a very real sense, that is the story of my grandfather, Nelson Mandela. I believe it is also my story. And I hope to convince you that it is your story as well.

Madiba and his colleagues in the African National Congress, Gandhi and his followers, Dr. Martin Luther King Jr. and all who marched alongside him—these people successfully broke the physical chains that existed under apartheid in South Africa, British rule in India, and Jim Crow segregation in the United States. The wrongheadedness and evil of apartheid and segregation were very clear. Black people were told, "No, you can't live in such and such a neighborhood or this or that house, because that's too close to the white people. No, you can't get on that bus. No, you can't use that tap or that toilet." These laws were wrong, and the judges, police, and prison guards were wrong to uphold them. If they truly did "serve with pride," certainly, they should look back with shame. Any law that violates the civil or human rights of another person should offend our natural sense of social justice. It should grind like sandpaper on our conscience, and I think it does, but we get very good at ignoring it.

"To be free is not only to cast off one's chains," my grandfather said. "It's to live in a way that respects and enhances the freedom of others."

When my grandfather and so many others fought for civil rights around the world and broke free from those physical chains of apartheid and segregation, it was very easy to identify who the enemy was. But in today's world, there is a new fight for young Africans—and for many young people around the world—and that is to break the mental chains that still exist. It's a lot harder to break the mental chains because you cannot touch them. They're not tangible. You cannot point them out. These chains exist within your mind, but they can be stronger than iron. Every link is forged by an act of injustice, large or small. Some are inflicted by the world; others we inflict on ourselves. Bob Marley sings about mental chains in "Redemption Song" and reminds you that the only one who can emancipate you is yourself.

As I travel the world, I hear young brothers and sisters talk about the "American dream"—a big house with a swimming pool and posh furniture and a servant—and I recognize that place as a jail. I hear talk, talk, talk on adverts and reality TV shows, nattering constantly about that narrow vision of worth and wealth, and I can't help but contrast that with the young African in Monrovia whose dream is to have a library, or the child in Syria whose dream is to go to a school with a roof, or the young black man in the United States who's attacked for simply saying, "My life matters." In them and in you—and in myself, because my grandfather opened my eyes to it—I see the new generation who will rewrite the world.

"Sometimes it falls on a generation to be great," Madiba said. "*You* can be that great generation. Let your greatness blossom."

I WAS BORN IN Soweto in December 1982. My parents had a turbulent marriage. Two strong personalities, both good people, but they struggled to make their family work in a situation that was overwhelmingly stacked against them. When I was two, my parents left Soweto because life there had become difficult as a result of the police harassment and protest violence in black neighborhoods. We went to live with Grandma Evelyn—my father's mother—in Cofimvaba, a tiny town on the Eastern Cape, where she owned a grocery store. This was a rural area with big stretches of farmland. We routinely shared the road with cows and chickens as we walked to school.

Grandma Evelyn was a staunch Jehovah's Witness, so reading the Bible was a daily event, morning and night. Before breakfast, she did a little ten-minute devotional. In the evening, before dinner, it would go on for about forty-five minutes. On Saturday and Sunday, Grandma Evelyn attended services at the Temple Hall. After one interminable three-hour service, I told her, "I never want to do that again." Grandma Evelyn laughed and said, "That's fine." She knew I was getting more than my share at home.

Life was pleasant and orderly at Grandma Evelyn's. She was the boss, but both my parents were there. My dad managed Grandma Evelyn's grocery store, and he always let me come in and get chips, candy, or chocolate or whatever I wanted. Sometimes he'd send me to buy cigarettes for him, which made me feel like a big kid. On my seventh birthday, Dad bought me a sheep, and we slaughtered and barbecued it, and I'd never eaten anything so delicious. This was a good moment for my mom and dad. They were together, young and healthy, and we were a happy family. During the holidays, my dad's sister Makaziwe (I call her Auntie Maki) came to visit with my cousins Dumani and Kweku. Kweku was three years younger than me, but we had a lot of fun together.

Everyone spoke isiXhosa. That was my first language,

the language I still love. In the movie *Black Panther*, the people of the make-believe world of Wakanda speak isiXhosa, the true-life language my granddad and I grew up with, so there's been some curiosity about it since the film came out and obliterated box office records on a global scale. I was so happy to see this spark ignite, to have people see the true beauty and power of Africa and hear my native language spoken around the world. It's a very theatrical language that incorporates clicks and growls and musical inflection like no other language on Earth. It requires the whole body, the jaw, not just the tongue.

The traditional Xhosa song "Qongqothwane"—a song people sing at a wedding to wish the happy couple a prosperous union—was made popular in the 1960s by Miriam Makeba. Europeans called it "The Click Song" because their language lacks the distinct percussive consonant that happens in isiXhosa. It's a tonal language, so a syllable means one thing when it's high and something completely different when it's low. You don't see the difference when it's spelled out. You have to live this language to truly understand it.

I started learning English when I was seven and moved to Durban with my father. I don't know why my mom didn't move there with us. I just remember that she wasn't there, and if I asked too many questions about it, I got a smack. Dad and I stayed with the family of Walter Sisulu, an African National Congress (ANC) activist who was in prison with my granddad. His wife, Albertina Sisulu, a nurse and an ANC freedom fighter, was Grandma Evelyn's cousin and best friend. People call her "Mother of the Nation," but to me, she was always Mama Albertina. Mama Albertina took me under her wing. Grandmotherly and fierce at the same time, she made a home for seven kids and several adults. We had to share everything, and it was crowded, but everyone was basically cool and there was always food, something I didn't appreciate until later. The adults were all involved in the ANC, so the children were surrounded by that vibe—the rhetoric, the passion, the determination—and inevitably, that became second nature to us. We experienced the chokehold of apartheid daily, so we thought about things like freedom and responsibility on a level most kids aren't exposed to so early in life.

Durban was home to a lot of South Africans of Indian descent—more Indians than any other city outside of India—because of the way the Group Areas Act shuffled "Asians" and "nonwhites" into certain areas during apartheid. So in Durban, I went to a Muslim school with mostly Indian students. I was the only black kid in my class, so it was pretty tough. All I could do was be tougher than the bullies. There was no use tattling or complaining. The grownups in the house had their own troubles.

I was relieved when Mom came back and took me to live with her brother in a relatively decent area of Soweto. The house was tiny, but there was running water and a two-burner stove, and most important, Mom was there. I missed my dad, but I liked the Catholic school in Johannesburg. I stayed with people from my mother's family for a while, and then I stayed with my father's family. Sometimes it was me and my dad, sometimes me and my mom. My parents were together now and then, but their relationship was starting to get violent. Sometimes I was scared, sometimes hungry. I remember being sent to knock on the neighbor's door to see if they had anything I could eat for supper.

For a while, I was sent to stay with Mama Winnie and her family, who could slightly better afford to feed me. Winnie Mandela was known far and wide in South Africa, my grandfather's second wife and a firebrand activist in the ANC. The government kept their eye on her. During the years that Madiba was in prison, they arrested and tortured her, which I suppose was their backhanded way of torturing my granddad, who had to sit there in Robben Island and know there was nothing he could do to help her. Being treated that way didn't bend her will at all. If anything, it made her and the rest of the ANC more determined. Anyone with the last name Mandela was subject to scrutiny and harassment by the government, so all these grownups had to create safe havens for themselves and their kids. We kids, for the most part, just went where we were told to go and made the best of it.

Mama Winnie lived on the corner of Vilakazi Street and Ngakane in Soweto, just up the street from Archbishop Desmond Tutu. That place is now a museum called Mandela House. It was declared a national heritage site in 1999. I haven't been there for a very long time, and it's strange to think of tourists going there to view the rooms we crammed into and the toilet we flushed with a bucket of water. I remember it as a place where I was singularly unhappy, but I didn't complain. I was grateful to have a roof over my head and food in my mouth, but I missed my parents terribly and got a strong vibe that I wasn't exactly welcome in the already crowded house. I kept sneaking back to my dad's house, which was just over the hill, so eventually, Dad let me come back to live with him. Later on my mom came to live there too, but my parents fought bitterly. After my baby brother Mbuso was born, they were seriously scraping for enough money to survive.

By the time I was ten, I'd grown used to this

underlying feeling of unease in my life, but I always
knew that I had people who loved me. Auntie Maki went
to live in the United States for a few years, getting her
PhD in anthropology from the University of Massachu-
setts, so Kweku was gone, and I missed hanging out with
him, but I ran with a good crew of friends in Jo'burg. I
went to a Catholic school, Sacred Heart College, which
had opened its doors to black children—children of all
races, actually—after the Soweto uprising on June 16,
1976. On that day, black South African high school students went out to protest a movement that had installed
Afrikaans as the language of instruction in schools
throughout the region. Their march was met with hor-
rifying brutality. The police who mowed these children
down with semi-automatic weapons reported the number of dead as 176, but in truth, the death toll was much
higher—some say as high as six or seven hundred with
more than a thousand wounded. The true numbers
can never be known, because police ordered doctors to
report all bullet wounds so that the wounded children
could be prosecuted, and the doctors got around that by
reporting injuries such as "abscesses" and "contusions"
instead of the actual gunshots and bludgeoning.

The violence rose and fell like a tide for several
hours, and all that night, armored vehicles called Hippos
prowled the streets. The Hippo was a familiar sight in

many black neighborhoods in Soweto and Johannesburg. Its unmistakable bulk was painted bright yellow with a blue stripe. Hippos were designed to drive over land-mines, so driving over protesters presented very little difficulty. As many as ten infantrymen could ride inside and leap out the back end as needed, but the Hippo's double machine gun turret was intimidating enough that it was rarely necessary for the occupants to debus. The day after the uprising, a force of fifteen hundred police officers poured in, carrying stun guns and automatic rifles. The South African Army was on standby to back them up, if it came to that. The uprising was effectively put down, but things would never be the same.

Sacred Heart College responded to all this by plac-ing an advert welcoming all races to the school. It was one of the first schools to do this, so many members of the African National Congress sent their children there. The ANC was one big family during those years. As children, we didn't understand the grave danger we were in, but the mamas were vigilant and smart. They knew their best hope was to support and protect each other. The grandchildren of Walter Sisulu and Jacob Zuma, ANC members who were in prison at Robben Island with my grandfather, were my friends, and we all attended Sacred Heart, which was in Observatory, a suburb about ten minutes from our house.

My friends and I heard stories about the Soweto uprising and other pitched battles between protestors and police. We played at stick fighting—Police and Protestors instead of Cops and Robbers—acting out the violence we saw on television every day. We boasted that we would take on the whole army if it came anywhere near our houses.

One autumn day in 1992—April is when summer ends, so this was probably May—my friends and I were out playing soccer, and we saw that a protest march was forming just up the street. We discussed the possible blowback. We were in primary school, about ten years old, so we still lived in fear of our mothers, grandmothers, and aunts. We weren't about to make any trouble that would incur their wrath. But we decided, "Hey, we're men! We're warriors!" Off we went, up the street.

It wasn't one of the huge marches, just a small but passionate group of eighty or maybe a hundred men and women in their twenties, singing, raising signs, and shouting in unison. We fell in step and marched with them, shouting and singing, and progressed two or three blocks before we saw the hulking yellow Hippo round the corner in front of us. There was a jerking motion from the turret. *Thok! Thok! Thok!* Tear gas canisters hissed over our heads. The next moment, everything was chaos. People screamed and scattered. People took off in every direction, blinded by the tear gas, desperate to get away from the Hippo. Some stumbled and fell. Others helped them up.

My friends and I, like a tight little flock of startled birds, peeled off together and beat feet toward home. We were only a few blocks from the street where we'd spent the morning playing. The Hippo roared and belched, pausing at the intersection, but we didn't slow down long enough to do more than glance over our shoulders. We ran, eyes streaming, throats choking, sinuses full of snot that seared like hot lava. We reached our front door, coughing and spitting, retching and reassuring each other that, no, no, we weren't crying—this was just the tear gas making our eyes water. We weren't terrified. Quite the opposite. We were elated! This was a proud moment. Now we were real soldiers. We knew the sting of tear gas.

This whole episode took place in a matter of minutes, and what is most remarkable about it is how unremarkable it was in the grand scheme of things. I doubt this incident even made it onto the evening news. This was a minor skirmish among a daily parade of minor skirmishes, neighborhood raids, and flurries of violent confrontation. It stands out particularly in my own memory only because it's The Story of the First Time I Felt the Burn of Tear Gas. It certainly was not the last.

This was life under apartheid. The police could roll into a black neighborhood and raid every house on the street whenever they pleased. People who objected were beaten and arrested. The only way the white minority could control the overwhelming black majority was to make them afraid, keep them poor, and grind them down, decade after decade, with an ugly fable about their inferiority. There were a few white people who hated apartheid and knew it was wrong, and clearly, when you look at the logistics and economics of it, apartheid was not sustainable. Those in power knew it would eventually end; they just didn't know how. In their mind, the only possible ending was terrible violence, because that's the only way they could see it continuing.

Meanwhile, cultural revolution was taking place on a global scale. My grandfather was arrested in August 1962 (facing charges of inciting workers' strikes and leaving the country without a passport) and released in February 1990. During the decades he was incarcerated, everything about the world had changed. Think of the difference between a child watching *Howdy Doody* on a black and white TV and a child watching *Ren & Stimpy* on a computer. Think of the difference between Chubby Checker doing "The Twist" and Dr. Dre dropping "The Chronic." The Beatles happened. The Vietnam War happened. Integration became the law of the land in the United States and Europe. MTV became a thing. Michael Jackson and Prince were being played at dance clubs from Soweto to Sweden. The Iron Curtain fell. The Soviet Union crumbled. The Berlin Wall came down. A full-on cultural revolution had rewritten the world, led by artists and musicians, poets and club kids, punkers and iron-blood orphans, a new generation empowered by a tornado of technological advances.

By the time the late 1980s rolled around, the white South African government was being loudly condemned by pretty much the whole planet. Progress was upon them, and they knew it, but they were terrified. What would happen if the white government removed its boot from the neck of the black population—which happened to outnumber the white population ten to one? How could people who'd been so oppressed, so abused, respond with anything but righteous wrath? They knew Mandela had great influence, and he consistently called for reconciliation and forgiveness, but what would happen to all his talk of peace when the opportunity for revenge was at hand? To believe in the power of forgiveness over the power of violence—that is a tremendous leap of faith. Foolishness, some would say.

There's an old Xhosa saying: *Idolophu egqibeleleyo iyakusoloko imgama.* Roughly translated, it means that Bakuba—the perfect city, Utopia, whatever you want to call it—is a long way off. No one's ever gotten there. But that doesn't mean it doesn't exist or that it can't exist in the future. It may take effort and struggle to get there, but it's still worthwhile to work toward that great vision of peace and equality.

When I met my grandfather, he was much closer to the end of his life than he was to the beginning. Twenty-seven years of memories, experiences, and opportunities had been taken from him, but his ideals were intact, along with his resolve and his baseline joy at being alive. He knew change was coming. In a BBC interview, he said, "It matters very little to me whether I see it or not, but it is definitely around the corner, and that's what motivates me."

My grandfather's release from prison in 1990 was a great moment. Most of the family was there to meet him when he came out, but there was time for little more than a brief handshake. He was swept into a throng of well-wishers, people celebrating wherever he went, thousands of people who loved him and had been waiting for even a fleeting opportunity to touch him or just get a glimpse of him as his car passed by. A great sense of elation swept over South Africa, but things didn't just change overnight. Apartheid was still very much in place. That battle was yet to be won.

My granddad used to tell a story about a great warrior.

There are different versions of this story, but essentially, this is how he told it: "Long ago, there was a brave bushman who fought the Afrikaners. Fought them long and hard. Even though they had guns, and he had only his bow and arrow. He saw his comrades fall, one after the other, until he was the only one left fighting, but still he kept on until he stood at the edge of a cliff with only one arrow left in his quiver. Well, the Afrikaners saw this, and they were impressed that he kept on fighting, even though he was the only one left. They raised the white flag and called out to him. 'Hey, we're all done here. We've defeated your people. There's nothing left for you to do but lay down your weapon and surrender. Come on over here, and we'll give you some food and water and call it a day.' The bushman warrior raised his bow, shot his last arrow, and jumped off the cliff."

Even as a kid, I knew this story was about that moment when you choose between self-preservation and commitment to a cause greater than yourself. At his trial in 1964, Madiba said: "I have fought against white domination, and I have fought against black domination. I have cherished the ideal of a democratic and free society in which all persons live together in harmony and with equal opportunities. It is an ideal which I hope to live for and to achieve. But if needs be, it is an ideal for which I am prepared to die." That wasn't big talk or bravado or hyperbole. He seriously believed the government was about to sentence him and his colleagues to be hanged as terrorists. This was the shiz-got-real, jump-off-the-cliff moment when they considered themselves *lucky* to be going to prison for the rest of their lives.

So they jumped off the cliff, fully prepared to die, and they fell for twenty-seven years. But then something amazing happened: Someone caught them. They found themselves in the arms of millions of people who believed in the ANC's vision of a free and democratic South Africa. They were prepared to die for it, but more important, they were prepared to live for it. They were prepared to stand up and show up, prepared to hold fast and sacrifice.

"Our people demand democracy," Madiba told a joint session of the United States Congress in 1990. "Our country, which continues to bleed and suffer pain, needs democracy."

2

Umthi omde ufunyanwa yimimoya enzima.

"The tall tree catches the hard wind."

The four years following Madiba's release from prison were some of the most turbulent years in the history of my country—and my family—as he rallied the full power and might of the people and labored to ensure an orderly election and peaceful transition away from apartheid. This left him very little opportunity to rebuild the relationships that had been severed when he went to jail.

Many times over the years, my grandfather told me that while he was in prison, his family suffered even more than he did. He also wrote about this later on in his autobiography, *Long Walk to Freedom*, saying how he was a man who had become a myth "and then that man returned home and proved to be just a man after all." Speaking as the father of the bride at my aunt Zindzi's wedding, he said that his children knew they had a father. They knew he would come back to them one day, and he did, but then he left them again, because now he was the father of a nation.

"To be the father of a nation is a great honor," said Madiba, "but to be the father of a family is a greater joy. It was a joy I had far too little of."

After the family visit to Victor Verster Prison, I didn't see Madiba again until 1993, when I was eleven years old. One afternoon, a big black BMW rolled into the down-at-heel neighborhood where I lived in Soweto and pulled up in front of the house on Vilakazi Street. The driver got out and told me to get in. I had never met this guy, of course, but he was Madiba's trusted longtime employee and friend, Mike Maponya. The way I heard it, Mike's uncle was driving my granddad around after he got out of prison, but the uncle couldn't accommodate

Madiba's intense schedule, so he threw the job to his nephew, Mike. Madiba liked him, and Mike ended up being Madiba's driver for more than twenty years. On this particular day, his job was to come and pick me up. Problem is, no one had told me about it.

"I was sent by your grandfather," Mike said. "He sent me to fetch you."

I was like, *Seriously?* Are you kidding me? A stranger rolls up out of nowhere and tells a little kid to get in his car? That's not happening.

"Your grandfather," Mike repeated. "You know who your grandfather is, right?"

I thought, *Yeah, I know my grandfather, but I don't know you, man.* My parents weren't home from work yet, and I hadn't seen my grandfather since he was released from prison three years earlier. I was not about to go anywhere with some random guy, but I'd been taught to respect my elders, so I said, "I'm sorry, sir. I can't go with you."

"What? Are you serious? Are you mad?" Mike opened the door and said quite insistently, "Kid. Get in the car."

I stood on the sidewalk trying to look tough. He got frustrated and started yelling at me.

"You want me to lose my job? Is that what you want?"

"No."

"Okay, then get in the car! We don't got all day."

"No."

We went back and forth for a while until he got the point that I was not getting in the car, and I was just big enough that putting me in the car against my will wasn't a good option. Eventually, he got back in the car, slammed the door, and drove away with all the neighbors staring after him through a cloud of yellow dust.

When my father got home, I told him what had happened. He listened without showing surprise or emotion. He just said, "If that man comes back, you go with him."

I had a million questions in my head. *Go with him where?* Last time I'd seen my grandfather, it was in that prison house that was hundreds of miles away. I knew he'd been let out of jail, but where did he live? How long would I stay there? How would I get home again? He was the president of the ANC now, so I figured he must have a pretty nice place. Would there be a swimming pool? What about a VCR? Or Nintendo! The Nintendo was entirely possible, and I was prepared to be totally okay with all of the above for however long I was supposed to hang out there, even for as long as a week or two.

A few days later, Mike rolled up in the big black BMW. No goodbyes. There was no one home for me to say goodbye to. I grabbed my backpack and got in the car. I figured that if I was to stay overnight, I would need my schoolbooks and some clean socks and a couple other things. As we drove out of the neighborhood, my friends paused their games in the street, pointing and hooting at the big black car. I don't remember everything about the drive, but I must have been feeling pretty large. My old neighborhood was a slum, basically, and as we approached Houghton, things got noticeably nicer. Mike pulled into the driveway at a huge white house, and an electronic gate slid sideways to let us in. He parked outside the garage, and I got out, not knowing what I was supposed to do.

"You hungry?" said Mike.

I nodded.

"Go on in." He gestured toward the door and followed me inside the kitchen, where ladies were busy doing kitchen lady things. One of them paused to look me up and down.

"Mama Xoli. Mama Gloria." Mike nudged me forward. "The grandson."

"You have a name?" said Mama Xoli.

"Ndaba."

She nodded and parked me at the table and set some supper in front of me. I don't remember exactly what it was, but I do remember feeling like it was the grandest feast I'd ever had. I was accustomed to comparatively humble fare like rice with ketchup and that sort of thing. The big kitchen at my grandfather's house was full of fresh fruit and vegetables. There was something that smelled amazing in a pot on the stovetop. I suspect every person in my family has some sweet or spicy memory set in that kitchen, and you can see many of those memories in Mama Xoli's cookbook, *Ukutya Kwasekhaya: Tastes from Nelson Mandela's Kitchen.* (*Ukutya kwasekhaya* means "food from home.")

Mama Xoli was a typical African woman, sturdy and kind. She was about as wide as a hippo, but that didn't stop her from dancing a little as she stirred a pot on the stove or chopped vegetables on the wooden cutting board. Her full name is Xoliswa Ndoyiya. She was raised on the Eastern Cape and learned to cook from her mother and grandmothers, so she was amazing at cooking all the traditional food my granddad loved, but she had also worked elsewhere for years, first for different families and then in a Jewish old folks' home, so she could make anything from kosher potato latkes to *umphokoqo*, which is like a crumbly, delicious mess of maize.

"My grandmother fed me her hopes and dreams along with this *umphokoqo*," she said whenever she set a bowl of it in front of me. "Tata Mandela says every time I make him *umphokoqo*, he remembers how his mother cooked it with love."

I'm convinced that was Mama Xoli's secret ingredient as well. Everything she ever cooked for me and my family, from the smallest sandwich to the greatest Christmas dinner, was full of love and stories.

"My mother made me eat *isidudu* for ten days after the birth of my children," she said, dishing up a fragrant pap made of pumpkin, curried cabbage, and liver. "With every spoonful I was receiving the strength and wisdom of all the women in my family."

She was always busy, but took time to squeeze my shoulder as she passed by and looked me in the eye when she talked to me, which made me feel like I could talk to her. She was fiercely protective of the Old Man and saw it as her solemn duty to make sure he was well fed and healthy enough to take the burdens of all South Africa on his shoulders.

"Tata is very, very busy," she said. "You don't make any trouble, understand?"

I nodded, not wanting to speak with my mouth full.

"He's a very important man, you know. He's president of the ANC. Standing for election. You'll see. Next year, he will be the president of South Africa, which is a very big place. He's got all kinds of crazy people upset about this and upset about that, so he doesn't need any trouble from little boys."

"Why are they upset?" I asked.

She sat down at the table, snapping peas into a bowl.

"Well," she said, "some people are upset because apartheid is over with. Some people are upset because it didn't get over with a long time ago. Some people think everything has got to change overnight, and some people think nothing should ever change at all. They get scared, and they blame Madiba."

"That's why you have the gate."

She looked at me sharply. "Yes," she said. But then she softened and added, "My father used to say, 'The tallest tree catches the harshest wind.'"

"What does that mean?" I asked.

"It means the greatest man gets the most people upset. If nobody's mad at you, you're probably not doing anything brave or important." Mama Xoli took her beans to the sink and ran water over them. "Most people—black and white—they love Madiba. They know it's hard to make changes, but it's good. It's like a little boy who has to go to school and work hard," she added pointedly, "and eat his vegetables, even if he doesn't like it."

When I was stuffed full of amazing food, Mama Xoli took me upstairs and showed me my room.

"I get to stay here?" I said.

She said, "Tata will talk to you about it."

She didn't tell me that a few days earlier, the Old Man had come to her and Mama Gloria and asked if

36

they would be onboard with the idea of helping him care for his grandson. She knew this was more than a temporary arrangement but figured he should be the one to explain that to me. I figured I was going to be here for a few days, and I was completely cool with that. I'd never in my life had a beautiful room like this. I'd never had a room to myself at all, let alone a room with a big bed with posh pillows and blankets. There was a TV on the dresser and a closet like a cavern. Outside the window, flowers and trees blossomed along the high wall that surrounded the house. I flopped down in front of the TV, feeling like I'd died and gone to heaven. I didn't know how long it would last, but I was going to enjoy myself while it did.

I was still lying there watching TV later that evening when my grandfather appeared at the door. "Ndaba! Welcome!"

I scrambled to stand in front of him, feeling very small. I'd almost forgotten how tall he was. In the years since we'd met at the prison, I'd seen him only on TV. He towered over me like that great tree Mama Xoli spoke of, but not in an intimidating or overbearing way. There was always a good feeling that came into the room with him. Like everything was all right now. My impression of my granddad, from the first day to the last, was much the same as the impression he left on the rest of the world—a paternal calm, defined by generosity and warmth. The deep lines at the corners of his eyes showed how much he liked to laugh. He always held himself straight and tall with a dignified posture and civil manners whether he was chatting with a child or a foreign head of state.

"How are you today?"

"I'm fine. Thank you."

He spoke to me in English, so I answered him in English.

"Good, good," he said. "Settling in all right? You have everything you need?"

I really wasn't sure, because I still had no idea why I was here or how long I was going to stay, but I didn't want to be any trouble, so I said, "Yes, Granddad."

"Good. Very good. I'm told you speak English very well."

I nodded. I didn't want to say anything that might be wrong.

"What about Afrikaans?"

"No!" I shook my head. Most of the people I knew mocked the ugliness of Afrikaans and said it was the language of the Dutch Imperialists. Why would anyone want to talk Afrikaans instead of Xhosa?

"You'll learn Afrikaans," he said. "It's very important."

It surprised me to hear this. I started to ask, "Why?"

but I stopped myself before it came out. I didn't want to sound impertinent.

"I studied Afrikaans when I was in school," said Madiba, "and when I was on the Island, I could write and speak Afrikaans better than the white prison wardens. They started coming to me for help, to translate and transcribe letters and documents. The prison director had to change the guards every six months, because he didn't want them to form friendships with me. 'Who's guarding Mandela? Him? No, he's too close. Send the one who knows he's the enemy.'"

He paused and studied my face to see if I was following. I wasn't.

"They were supposed to be my enemies," he said. "But if you learn your enemy's language, you have a great power over him. In order to defeat the enemy, you must work with him. He becomes your partner. Maybe even your friend. So you'll work on this in school. Learning Afrikaans. All right, Ndaba?"

"Yes, Granddad."

He asked me about my friends. He was warm and kind, as he always was, but still, the man was a stranger to me, and I was pretty overwhelmed by the situation, so I didn't volunteer a whole lot of information.

He finally said, "All right. We'll figure it all out as we go. Be in bed at ten o'clock."

"Yes, Granddad."

He turned to go, but before he went out the door, he cast a critical eye around the room and nodded toward my backpack on the floor by the bed. "I expect you to keep your room clean, Ndaba."

"Yes, Granddad."

"No matter how humble or grand your surroundings, orderliness is a matter of self-respect."

"Yes, Granddad."

"All right. Good night, Ndaba."

"Good night, Granddad."

"You're sure there's nothing else you need?"

"Well…"

He smiled down at me and said, "If there's something you need, say so."

I smiled up at him and said, "Nintendo."

3

Umntana ngowoluntu.

"No child belongs to one house."

To understand The Story of Ndaba and His Grandfather, you must understand how African families function (or dysfunction) as an extended, inclusive group. Monogamy is relatively new in Xhosa culture. The "traditional" family of husband, wife, two kids, and a dog was not our tradition. That concept arrived with missionaries and colonialism.

Polygamy and arranged marriages were more in keeping with the old ways. My great-grandfather, Nkosi
Mphakanyiswa Gadla Mandela, principal counselor to
the King of the Thembu, had four wives and thirteen
children, but my granddad made the conscious decision
to marry only one woman at a time, and all three of his
marriages were for love.

Madiba's first wife was my grandmother, Evelyn.
They were married in 1944 and divorced in 1958 as his
involvement with the ANC became more and more dangerous. Their first son, my uncle Thembi, who had two
children, Ndileka and Nandi, was tragically killed in a
car accident during the early years of my grandfather's
imprisonment. Their second son, my father, Makgatho,
was twelve years old when Madiba went to jail, and Aunt
Makaziwe was ten. Madiba had married his second wife,
Mama Winnie, in 1958, and they had two daughters, my
aunts Zenani and Zindzi, who were not even school age
when their father was taken. My older brother Mandla
is the son of my father's first wife, Rose. After Dad and
Rose were divorced, he married my mother Zondi, a
Zulu, who had me and my two younger brothers, Mbuso
and Andile. My cousin Kweku, whose mom is Auntie
Maki, is as close as a brother, and I can't even name
all of our great-aunts and great-uncles, cousins, second
cousins, in-laws, and current or former spouses and

offspring. The point is this: We are all family. Each and every one.

African families are exhausting and noisy, full of love and music, prone to heated arguments and great loyalty. Xhosa and Zulu women are famously strong and beautiful. They're fiercely protective of their children, and everyone in the family is fiercely protective of the elderly, so it makes sense to be practical about it and agree that you're welcome at my table, I'm welcome at your table. Your kids are welcome to sleep over and share the room with my kids. Naturally, jealousy or petty differences crop up from time to time, but whatever it is, it's not as important as family.

Millennials think they've come up with something brand new when they declare "love is love" and say, "There is no single definition of family, or at least not one definition that everyone in the world agrees on, so we must set aside our learned notions of what a family should look like and create families that are the healthiest, most loving environment possible for ourselves and our children." But this is how African families have operated for dozens of generations. It's nice that the rest of the world is finally catching up to us.

Operating as an extended family is very much in keeping with tradition, but beyond that, the Mandela and ANC families had to depend on each other through decades of terrible danger and uncertainty. So despite the extraordinary circumstances, it didn't strike me as unusual when I was sent to stay with my grandfather. I figured I'd be there for a while, a few days or weeks or even months maybe, but eventually my dad would come fetch me or someone would drive me back to my parents' house, and life would go on as before. And sure enough, my father did show up at Madiba's house after only a few days. I don't recall exactly what I was doing when he got there. Probably playing Sega.

The Nintendo—that Holy Grail of video games in 1994—was still just out of reach, but the Sega was all mine. "Ask and ye shall receive," as Grandma Evelyn used to say. During that first week, I saw very little of my grandfather, who was extremely busy, running for president of a country on the brink of civil war and all that, but I had quickly discovered that he was kind and generous and eager to make me feel welcome. Within a day or two, I had been provided with clothes, shoes, socks, underwear—all kinds of brand new things that smelled like the store they came from and had never been worn by my big brother or cousins. I had my own dresser to put all these things in, and if I slopped something on my shirt while I was wolfing down my lunch, I could toss that shirt in a hamper, and someone would come and take it away and wash it, and it would reappear, clean and freshly folded, rather like in The Story of the Zulu Woman and the Accommodating River. This woman tosses a handful of dirt into a magic river and says, "River, give me a clay pot." *Whoosh*, a nice clay pot washes up on the shore.

So a few days after I came to my granddad's for what I thought was a visit, my dad arrives at the house in Houghton, and I'm thinking, *Ah, well, that was fun while it lasted*. My only big concern was whether I would be allowed to take the Sega home with me. My dad went into Madiba's office and closed the door. While they were talking, I went up to my room to stuff my new clothes into my backpack. I was sorry to leave this wonderful place, and I would miss Mama Xoli's cooking, but I was glad to see my dad and anxious to get home to my mom and baby brother. I was a big boy of eleven and not a mama's boy at all, but it was strange not hearing her voice in the morning. I felt I should be there to take care of her, because sometimes my parents fought, and things got out of hand. I felt I should be there to care for Mbuso, because sometimes my parents drank too much, and the baby's crying made me feel nauseous and uneasy. The thought of him crying and me not being there made me feel even worse.

I was ready to go when my father came in and sat on my bed. He said, "Madiba is a great man. It's important for his family to accomplish great things. I can still make something of my life. I can still be a lawyer. I have to focus on my education." He said Madiba was sending him to study law at the university in KwaZulu-Natal. Apparently there was a look on my face like I didn't understand, so he put it bluntly: "You live here now."

He may have hugged me before he left. I don't recall. I can be certain there was no great show of emotion. That was not our way. I didn't ask questions. I didn't cry. I did as I was told. I unpacked my bag and put my things away carefully so my room would be tidy when my grandfather came up to say goodnight.

I didn't hear from my mother for a long time. She didn't call me or write to me, and though no one expressly said anything about it, I got a vibe that I shouldn't expect her to show up for a visit. My granddad told me later that she was studying social work some- where. Elsewhere. Somewhere far away from my father and from me. No one explained to me that she and my dad were both struggling with alcoholism. The older generation considered these topics inappropriate for discussion, and they were certainly not to be discussed with children.

For the next several years, my parents were not part of my story. This is something I struggled with later in my life. When I was old enough to understand how this separation affected their relationship and came to understand the role my grandfather played in that decision, I struggled to forgive him. I tried to cut him some slack, knowing how deeply it had wounded him to come out of prison and realize that he had missed a lifetime of parenting his children. He came into a position of power and wealth, and naturally, he wanted to help them—I know that was his good intention—but I think he was wrong to separate my parents this way. My mother was really left behind, if I'm to be honest. For me at the time, it was as if she just disappeared.

Rather like the Zulu woman at the river.

You see, that accommodating river seems like a super deal at first, so the Zulu woman keeps going back. She asks for bigger things, and the river exacts greater and greater sacrifices. The pot for a boat. The boat for a house. Finally she says, "River, give me back the child I lost long ago." And the river says, "Cut out your heart and give it to me."

I suppose the main message of the old story is similar to the Western saying that warns you to "be careful what you wish for," but now that I have children of my own, I understand on another level what this story says about the preciousness of African children. The mother, without hesitation, cuts out her own heart for her child. There's no doubt in my mind that my mother loved me that much. I'm certain she believed she was doing the right thing sending me to live with Madiba, and as painful as it is for me to say it, it *was* the right thing. Sometimes doing the right thing for your child is hard. Sometimes it cuts your heart out. But if my mother had come to fetch me from my granddad's house, I would have had a very different life, and it would not have been better than the life I've had.

It took me many years to make sense of all this. It wasn't until I was in college myself, studying political science in Pretoria, that I was able to connect my mother's broken heart to the big picture of apartheid, a political system that forced black families into this type of situation. When Madiba became president of South Africa, the laws changed, yes—everything changed on paper—but black South Africans had been deprived of educational, social, political, and economic opportunities for several generations; he knew it would take several generations to overcome the legacy of oppression. His own family was a prime example.

Madiba's own father died when he was young, and then he was deprived of the opportunity to be a father to his own children. Then my dad, who never knew his grandfather, grew up without his father, so that relationship was set back another generation. There was no lack of love or intelligence or ability. These men were totally willing to be there and work hard for their families, but the opportunity to have a father and be a father was taken away from them. So it goes to the next generation and the next one after that: me and my son. This little dude—my Lewanika—I would cut out my heart for him in a second. One hundred percent. But I know from experience that this is not enough. My love for him is not enough; he needs *me*. My voice. My strong arms. My laughter. My example. He needs to see me stand fully present in my own life and to feel me be fully present in his. That's where he begins to understand his value: in the family, then in the community, then in the nation, and then in the world. And it's a challenge, because he and his sister live with their mother, my former girlfriend. I have to mindfully, purposefully choose to spend time with my kids. I have to make it a priority, and I struggle with the logistics of that, so I understand how difficult it can be, but I take the responsibility seriously.

This generation of African men—my generation—has the power to turn the course of that unforgiving river. We, as fathers, could literally re-create the culture of this continent if we so choose. I'm not minimizing the importance of mothers when I say this. Not at all. I'm just calling out my brothers, speaking from what I know, and asking them to really think about what it means to be good fathers, to have good fathers, and to raise good fathers—to create a culture that values father-hood and a socioeconomic system that serves families by collectively refusing to place individuals in positions of powerlessness.

I recognize that I have lived an extraordinarily privileged life. I understand that my grandfather believed that I and my brothers and cousins and all African children would benefit from the example of self-respecting African adults and an elevated international opinion of Africa as a homeland. I believe the same thing myself, but I think there's a way to achieve those broader goals without leaving families behind. I wish my grandfather had found a way to help my parents move forward together.

YOU MAY HAVE HEARD the expression, "It takes a village to raise a child." The Xhosa have their own version: *Akukho mntwana ungowendlu enye.* "No child belongs to one house." One would hope that the logical extension of this is: "Every child belongs to every house." Which is to say, we all share responsibility for the care and feeding of all the children in this world.

I missed my mom and dad, but the good part of my childhood came after I went to live with the Old Man. Mama Xoli cared for me like a mother hen. Auntie

Maki had returned from the United States, so I spent holidays with her family, and Kweku and I tore around having fun like we did when we were little. Life with my grandfather settled into a disciplined daily routine. I was expected to behave myself, do well in school, and keep my room clean. Madiba was a man of extraordinary will who'd spent almost three decades living a very rigidly structured life. Self-discipline was like a religion in his house, and that was something very new to me. Grandma Evelyn ran a pretty tight ship, but she was also warm and generous with affection. I don't remember much in the way of hugs or sentimental words from my granddad during that first couple of years. I think he was as perplexed by me as I was by him.

Still it was hard to complain. For the first time in my life, I had my own room and a lot of other things my friends were quite envious of. I arrived at school in a private car instead of a taxi—and South African taxies are not like yellow cabs. In South Africa, a taxi is like a minibus with fifteen or sixteen people jammed into it. The private car was driven by a guy I called Bhut, a word that essentially means "bro" but older. This was a very nice change, and sometimes my friends were allowed to come home in the car with me after school to play games, watch videos, or swim in the pool.

My cousin Rochelle stayed with us in those early

days, but she was in her twenties and had a life of her own. I never asked why Mama Winnie wasn't there. I'd overheard enough adult conversation to know that her life was separate from the Old Man's. They weren't divorced yet, but the duties of First Lady were being carried out by Aunt Zenani and Aunt Zindzi, who came to Madiba's office when needed and accompanied him to various social and state events. Everyone who worked in my granddad's house loved him and felt privileged to be there—and no one hesitated to remind me what a privilege it was for me as well.

The ladies who prepared Madiba's meals took great pride in serving him their best work. He was very specific about the type of food he wanted to eat, and the kitchen staff was more than happy to accommodate him. My granddad adored tripe, chicken legs, and something called *amasi* in isiZulu or *maas* in Afrikaans. Mama Xoli made it by setting a jar of raw cow's milk on the window sill, letting it ferment until it separated into a layer of watery *umlaza* on top of the thick white *amasi* that was sort of like cottage cheese or plain yogurt. The *amasi* could be eaten right out of the jar or spooned over maize meal. My granddad liked it very sour. The sourer the better. Sometimes he'd have a taste, consider it for a moment, and then shake his head, and the ladies would put it back on the windowsill to let it curdle even further.

I had breakfast and lunch in the kitchen with Mama Gloria and Mama Xoli, but most evenings, Madiba and I sat down together, just the two of us, at seven o'clock sharp, to eat our dinner at the long table in the formal dining room. He always sat at the head of the table, of course, and I sat on the side in the seat closest to his. During that first year, dinner conversation was sparse and always in English.

He'd say, "Good evening, Ndaba. How was school today?"

I'd say, "It was okay."

He'd say, "Good. Good."

He rang a little bell when he was ready for the food to be brought in. Not in an imperious way, just to let people know we were ready. He saw me eyeing that bright silver bell the first few days, and then one evening he gave me a wink and said, "You want to give it a try?" I nodded. He slid the bell across the table to me, and I gave it a solid *ding-a-ling*. In came the chef with our dinner, and somehow that felt very satisfying to me, like I was the founder of the feast or something. Madiba laughed and clapped my shoulder and thanked everyone for our supper, which we ate in silence. It wasn't an uncomfortable silence. We were together, and that was good. My granddad was happy to have a family member sitting there with him. I was happy to have enough to eat. Everybody's cool.

Sometimes someone would bring a phone to the table. Invariably the caller was a very important person calling from someplace where it was still business hours. Madiba would set down his fork, dab his mouth with his napkin, and then take the phone. "Hello! How are you today?"

He always greeted the caller with the same big smile. It didn't matter who they were or that they couldn't see the smile. It could be heard. It could be felt. I have no doubt. At the time—eleven years old, my mind firmly on soccer and video games and MTV—I wasn't listening, and if I had been, I would have understood very little, but it occurred to me years later, as I was studying the history of this period, how truly contentious some of these phone calls must have been. Some of those callers were angry, bitter, and afraid, so it blows me away now to think of him greeting every one of them with respect and warmth.

In April 1994, Madiba voted for the first time in his life. On May 10, he became the first black president of South Africa.

"Let there be justice for all," he said in his inaugural

address. "Let there be peace for all. Let there be work, bread, water and salt for all."

Black South Africans were free at last, and my grandfather was being called the Father of the Nation, but as Coretta Scott King reminds us, "Freedom is never really won; you earn it and win it in every generation." The bitter legacy of apartheid carved deep ruts in that road: long-ingrained racism, inner-city violence and poverty, a rampant AIDS epidemic, and intense political pressure from both sides. The eyes of the world were on us, and there were huge expectations—positive and negative. There was unimaginable pressure on Madiba—far beyond anything I understood at the time, but he kept his cool, even at home in private, no matter how exhausted he was.

When he did crack down on me, he scolded proper. You felt that growl like thunder. This was something far worse than having him be mad at me; he was disappointed. I'd be chilling in the lounge in front of the TV and hear this deep, rumbling voice from upstairs.

"*Ndaba*. Come and clean your room."

That was my cue to get up there and tidy up while he stood in the door, delivering a stern talk about personal responsibility. He made me keep my room tidy, and he kept his own room tidy—made his own bed, everything—despite the fact that household staff would have been happy to do it. He was strict, and that caused some friction between us over the years.

There is one particular incident I must remember to tell my own children someday: I lost my school jersey and needed money to buy another one. I was free to ask him for anything I wanted—video games, books, a Sony Walkman—and that was fine. He might say yes or he might say, "No, I think you have enough games for now." But there was no problem with asking. This situation was different; I was asking him to replace something because I had failed to take proper care of it. So I went to my cousin Rochelle first.

"Rochelle, may I please have forty rand?"

She rolled her eyes. "Psshh! No. If you need something, ask Granddad."

"I can't."

"Why not?"

"Because—forget it."

I went to the kitchen. "Hey, Mama Xoli? Can you take me to get a new school jersey?"

"Why?"

"Because..."

"Did you outgrow the old one?" She eyed me up and down. "You don't look like you've grown so much since yesterday."

I thought of several excuses. It got torn when I was

climbing a fence. It was stolen during soccer practice. A dog ate it. But I knew she'd see through that in a hot second.

"I lost it," I said.

"Uh-huh. Well, you'd better go tell him."

I went down the hall and paused at the door to Madiba's office where he was sitting in a chair reading. "Granddad?"

"Ndaba." He smiled and motioned me to come in. "How are you today? How was school?"

"It was okay. But...Granddad, I lost my jersey. I need another one."

"Oh, Ndaba."

"I'm sorry, Granddad."

After the stern talk about personal responsibility, reminding me how many people in the world had nothing and no one to ask if they needed the most basic necessities, he said, "I'll tell Rochelle to go with you and buy it tomorrow. And I expect you to take better care of this one."

Head bent by shame, I said, "I will. I'm sorry, Granddad."

"All right. Go to bed now."

I went to my room, feeling like the exchange had gone as well as it could have. "No blood, no foul," as they say. But a few weeks later I lost my jersey again.

I was shaking in my shoes when I had to go tell him, trying to come up with any possible Plan B. Run away. Go to a different school. Try to find any conceivable way to blame it on someone else. Try to look as pathetic as possible and stir sympathy.

"Granddad?"

"Ndaba..." When he glanced up, I suppose he noticed I was practically shrinking inside out. "What is it?"

"I'm sorry," I said wretchedly. "I lost my jersey again."

There was no sympathy. He was straight up furious. The personal responsibility talk went to another level, and at the end of it, he didn't offer up Rochelle getting me another replacement.

"Clearly," he said, "you didn't take it seriously when I told you to take better care of this one. That's how much you appreciate your home and all the things you have here—your clothes, your games, your room that I must tell you every day, 'Clean this room, Ndaba. Pick up your clothes.' Well, you know what? Tonight you sleep outside."

I stood there, gobsmacked.

"Go outside!" he thundered. "You're not welcome in this house tonight."

What could I do? I slunk down the hall and out the door. The shadows were already long. It was dusk.

It would be dark soon. The yard was surrounded by a high wall. I figured if bad guys tried to climb over it, the security people would come out and stop them. Theoretically. I found a fairly comfortable spot on the grass beneath a blue guarri tree, but I wondered if there might be snakes in the sneezewood trees and wisteria surrounding the pool. It got dark. The heat of the day faded. I sat there shivering, arms hugged tight around my knees. I just about jumped out of my skin when I heard Mama Xoli call my name from the kitchen door.

"Ndaba?"

Startled but relieved, I ran to meet her as she walked out under the yard light. I assumed she'd come to take me inside for supper. That was not the case.

She handed me a blanket and said, "Madiba asked me to give this to you."

I tried to say "thank you," but there was a lump in my throat. He was serious. He was going to make me stay out here all night in the cold with no food and probably poisonous snakes and potential thugs and assassins maybe climbing over the wall. Mama Xoli went back inside, and I swallowed hard. My eyes were burning, but allowing myself to cry wouldn't have done me any good. I wasn't one to cry, even at that age. Maybe for something physical, like the time my friends and I faced down the tear gas–belching Hippo, but this was a thousand times worse than that, because I was alone, and I'd made my granddad so angry, and sooner or later I'd have to face him again. So be it. Come what may, I was not going to cry. Because a Xhosa man endures. This is what we say when we greet each other.

"Hello," a guy says. "How are you?"

"*Ndi nya mezela*," says the other guy. *I am enduring.*

I found a good spot to sit down and wrapped the blanket around my shoulders. Birds settled in the trees, whistling softly every time a breeze moved through the branches. After a while, I saw Mama Gloria inside the kitchen window, washing dishes and hanging the pots and pans. Supper was over. My stomach was hollow with hunger. I would have been glad for a bowl of the old rice with ketchup. Beetles chirped in the hedges. Somewhere far away a dog was barking, begging to be let in. I started to drift off but jerked awake when I heard heavy footsteps coming toward me. I scrambled to my feet and saw the Old Man crossing the lawn.

"Ndaba?"

"Yes, Granddad?"

"If you ever lose your jersey again," he said, "you really will sleep outside. Do you understand?"

"Yes, Granddad."

"Let's go in."

He headed back toward the house, and I fell in beside him, trying to keep up with his great long stride.

"My father loved and respected his children, but he did not spare the rod. He maintained discipline." He opened the kitchen door and shooed me into the entry-way. "Go inside and have dinner and then go to bed."

I was never so glad to be at that kitchen table. And I never lost another school jersey. Since Lewanika and Neema came along, I hear myself saying a lot of the same things my granddad said to me when I was a boy. In fact, Lewanika's mother called me not long ago and said, "I don't know how he managed it, but your son has already lost his school jersey."

I laughed. He was just starting his first year at big boy school, so that didn't take long.

"What's so funny?" she asked.

"Nothing. Tell him if it happens again, he'll sleep outside."

4

Kuhlangene isanga nenkohla.

"The wonderful and the impossible sometimes collide."

The Xhosa Story of the Tree That Would Not be Grasped resembles the European story of Cinderella. The similarity between two tales from utterly different cultures makes me wonder: Was one inspired by the other, or is there a common ground that brings this fable close to home for all of us? Do we all share an innate sense of justice and injustice that causes these stories to resonate like a tuning fork?

In the Xhosa story, beautiful Bathandwa's mother dies, leaving her to live as a servant at the mercy of the Second Wife and two unkind stepsisters. A tree that contains the mother's spirit grows up by a river. A magic bird flies out of it and says to the king, "You should have a contest. Whoever can put their arms around this awesome tree should be given a great fortune, and if the winner happens to be a girl, she should marry your son." The king likes this idea, so the contest is on, and everyone in the kingdom shows up, including the unpleasant Second Wife and cruel stepsisters. Apparently, they're not so bright, because they don't recognize Bathandwa. (Let's just agree that she's disguised herself or something, because it's details like this that make the difference between a fairy tale and something that simply makes no sense, which is why the African version of any story will go off on lengthy tangents to explain random details.) So one after another, contenders wrap their arms around the tree—the strongest men, the most agile women—but the tree twists away from them, refusing to be grasped by anyone but Bathandwa, the tree spirit's beloved daughter who was cast aside and abused.

I like the African spin on this old fable. My little daughter, Neema, is feisty and imaginative, so I'd much rather tell her about a heroine who drives a team of oxen than a princess who rides in a golden pumpkin. I suppose you could say the "fairy godmother" in the Xhosa folktale is the spirit of the girl's mother made manifest in the tree—a growing, living tower of strength—which is certainly an apt description of my mother and grandmothers. While Cinderella has a "happily ever after" ending, the Xhosa tale goes on to spin a fantastical web of murder and magic and (depending on who's telling it) some adult matters. But in both stories, justice prevails in the end. The cruel stepmother and stepsisters come to a gruesomely bad end. Maybe this reveals another difference between the two cultures; African children were spared no gore. We were not protected from the facts of life and death. The place and time we grew up in made that impossible.

When my friends saw me ride on out of the slums of Soweto in a black BMW, I suppose they thought I was living a Cinderella story of my own. Without a doubt, my circumstances were remarkably improved, and in their imagination, I was living an easy life now. I think that may be the way the rest of the world viewed the end of apartheid. Throughout Europe and the Americas, apartheid was strongly condemned. Artists and musicians raised the awareness worldwide, and the whole world celebrated when Madiba became president of South Africa. I think a lot of people saw this as the happy ending, but we still struggle with difficult economic issues like land redistribution to this day.

One example of this is the American movie *Invictus*, which tells the story of the 1995 World Cup won by South Africa when I was twelve. The movie version plays out like this: The majority of black people thought the government should do away with all institutions that stood as artifacts from the era of apartheid, but Madiba was wise enough to see that it would be more powerful to compromise on a few things as a gesture of reconciliation to the white minority. One was the national anthem "Die Stem van Suid-Afrika" ("The Call of South Africa"), a stolid march glorifying the colonization of South Africa. Another was the Springboks, South Africa's national rugby team, which had had only one nonwhite player in its hundred-year history. In the movie, the Springboks win the World Cup, black people just have to get over themselves, and white people turn out to be pretty nice after all. During the climactic rugby match, Mandela's black and white bodyguards become buddies, a white lady and her black housekeeper hug each other in the stands, and friendly white cab drivers hoist a delighted black boy onto their shoulders in celebration of this newfound harmony between races. And they all live happily ever after, which is how you know it's a fairy tale. It wasn't so simple in real life.

Inzondo is the Xhosa word for hatred, but the word *ngcikivo* has a whole additional level of connotation. It's more like *contempt*—that deeply ingrained refusal to accept the humanity of another person, a stubborn blindness to their suffering, a self-comforting belief that they don't really matter. Racism on that level—whether it's legal, institutional, cultural, or personal—does not change in the course of a rugby match. Or a rugby season. Or a generation. I'm not sure it will ever go away completely. Perhaps the most we can hope for is to make it socially unacceptable and economically imprudent so people keep racist comments and actions to themselves. But I know this, as surely as I know my last name: *We have to try*. We have to call out racism when we see it— even when we see it in ourselves.

Madiba's response to contempt was compassion. Relentless compassion. Compassion that rolled over their hatred like a Hippo. He said more than once, "Nonviolence is a strategy." He referred to "the Gandhian strategy" of noncooperation and peaceful but unstoppable resistance. He wasn't a saint who loved everyone and wouldn't smack a flea. He was a judicious leader who understood the power of doing the right thing until it overwhelms the wrong thing. Overwhelming racism with love and mutual respect is an ongoing process in South Africa, as it is in the United States and Europe and everywhere else in the world, and we, as a world community, have a long way to go.

From time to time, I hear about an ugly incident of racism—something a white person does to a black person here in South Africa or an African American man being brutalized by the police in the United States—and it makes my heart sink. People get outraged, as they should, but think about how it was ten years ago when there was no social media and incidents like these were ignored, not even reported as newsworthy. It's rotten that these things still happen, but at least we're hearing about it now. I see some very clear parallels between the liberation movement that occurred in South Africa and what's happening now in the United States with the Black Lives Matter movement and football players "taking a knee" in a peaceful but very public protest. There is an awakening taking place—about racism, about sexism, about xenophobia. The general consensus has shifted from "that's just the way it is" to "that's not acceptable." It's a starting point. Dr. Martin Luther King Jr. and Barak Obama both liked to quote Theodore Parker, a transcendentalist minister who fought for the liberation of slaves in America in the 1800s: "The arc of the moral universe is long, but it bends toward justice." I believe that's true, but I'm not as patient as the Old Man. Sometimes I feel like we could all be bending a little harder.

When I was in grade three, one of eight black boys in my class, my good friend Selema started a gang that we called *Bendoda* (the Gents). We had matching pens and wore matching badges on our lapels. Selema was like a little Napoleon. He was tiny, but he was tough. Michael Jackson was everything back then, and we fancied ourselves to be very much like the agile dudes in the "Bad" video. During recess and after school, we fought with the white boys, who had their own crew, and most of the time, we won. We chased them up trees, and all they could do was try to spit on us from up there, because they were afraid to come down. It was crazy. We frequently ended up in the principal's office, but our parents would show up, and they always had our backs.

Selema's mom was Barbara Masekela. Before she became head of the ANC's Department of Arts and Culture, she taught English literature at Rutgers. (She was also the younger sister of the famous jazz musician, Hugh Masekela, and later on, after my granddad became president, she was his head of staff.) So the Gents would be in the principal's office with the white parents raining down trouble, and Mama Barbara would come in, and that was it. She'd shut them down with some hard truth about what it was like for these eight little black boys who were just trying to protect themselves.

I remember an essay I wrote in school that year. It said something like, "I want to have a nice car and a nice house, but I don't want to be rich. White people are rich." That's how it seemed to me at that age. I wanted what white people had, but I didn't want to be like them, and rugby was a white people thing. My friends and I had played soccer since we were little, but we never paid any attention to rugby. We grew up hearing various versions of the saying: "Rugby is a thug's game played by gentlemen. Soccer is a gentlemen's game played by thugs." We were cast as the thugs in that scenario, and we wanted to be rebels. All through our early years, we'd heard stories about our parents and their comrades in the ANC liberation movement, and for us, that was the epitome of cool: to be a rebel, to go against the system. In our minds, when we were children being raised in the crucible of apartheid, everything broke down to black against white. Madiba saw the struggle as justice against injustice, right against wrong, giving against greed, unity against division. These were the far more nuanced discussions that needed to take place. There were no simple answers, but the disconnect between people was not so stark.

The 1995 World Cup was the first rugby match I ever watched. I suspect it was a first for a lot of black people. I wasn't there; I saw it on TV with a few cousins and friends. For me, the thing that made it a special occasion was that my dad came over and watched it with us. I didn't know it at the time, but he'd been in and out of rehab. He was trying hard in school and in life. All I knew was that having him there made the rugby match a lot more of an event than it would have been otherwise. He thought it was exciting to have South Africa represent like that.

"Hey, one year of independence, and we made it to World Cup finals!" That sort of thing.

And it was fun to see Madiba on television, smiling in a Springbok jersey. He was the reason most black people were watching, and I believe this is what made the event important. When he stepped up as a leader who cared about all the people in his country, including the white minority, his clear intention was to make us one country. This was a Herculean undertaking that many people thought was impossible until Madiba stepped out onto the field and reminded us: *Kuhlangene isanga nenkohla*. The wonderful and the impossible sometimes collide.

F OR BOTH HUMANITARIAN AND strategic reasons, children were a priority for Madiba. Just a few weeks after he took office, he established the Presidential Trust Fund that laid the foundation for the Nelson Mandela Children's Fund, to which he donated R150,000 (about $12,000 American) every year. This was a third of his salary as president. When he made this announcement, he told parliament members, "The emancipation of people from poverty and deprivation is most centrally linked to the provision of education of quality."

The stripping away of opportunity from the vast majority of black people for generations left one of the deepest scars of apartheid, and the end of apartheid could not undo that damage. The memories were seared into us from earliest childhood. All around us was civil strife, domestic unrest, grinding poverty, and a sense of hopelessness that weighed our parents down. In the big picture, the Old Man saw education as part of the ongoing fight for the liberation of black people, their only avenue to economic and social equality. In the small picture, he saw me.

My granddad let me know from the start that he expected me to be an A student, which blew my mind, because I had always gotten Cs and Ds. Maybe a B here and there. He didn't dog me about my homework on a daily basis; he cared about results. I dreaded showing him my test papers and reports.

"You're smarter than this, Ndaba," he said. "You have

to do better. You're a Mandela. People expect you to be a leader. You should be getting the best marks in the class."

"Yes, Granddad."

Like any kid, I'm going to say that, but inside, I'm like, *Pssh! Whatever!* I didn't want to be a leader. I was proud of my bad boy vibe. I was getting quite tall and considered myself to be pretty smooth in social situations. I had zero interest in studying. I was happy to chill at the back of the class, playing pranks, copying other people's homework, and sailing by. I was smart enough to muddle through with passing marks on tests most of the time, and that was good enough for me. It was not good enough for Madiba. It irked him terribly to see anyone blow off their own potential, and it was especially frustrating that he couldn't seem to make me care about school. He was an extremely busy man with extremely high standards, and he certainly did not have time to keep a constant eye on a stubborn twelve-year-old, but my education was very important to him.

One evening at dinner, he informed me that I would be going to The Ridge School, a private prep school for boys. A boarding school. This was a bit of a gut punch. I'd settled into my new home and was basically pretty happy there, but the Old Man traveled a lot, so I was left in the care of Rochelle and Mama Xoli and the security guys. In retrospect, I understand why he thought I'd be better off boarding at The Ridge. Perhaps he thought I was lonely when he was gone, and I was sometimes, but I preferred to be lonely in my own room rather than lonely in the middle of a crowd of boys I didn't know.

"It's not far away," the Old Man said. "You'll come home every weekend."

I nodded. My stomach felt hollow and strange.

"You'll be responsible for your school uniform," he said. "You must keep it clean and pressed. You must apply yourself to your studies, Ndaba. You're a very intelligent boy, capable of top marks, and top marks are what I expect."

"Yes, Granddad."

He patted my hand firmly. "Don't be gloomy. You'll have fun. You'll play tennis and rugby."

Rugby, I cringed inside. *Awesome.*

The following Monday morning, the driver took me there instead of taking me to school at Sacred Heart. As we made our way through the city traffic, I thought about my friends arriving at school and wondering where I was. The driver turned in, past a wide iron gate in a long fieldstone wall, and I went through all the motions of orientation and registration. I received my uniform: a pale blue shirt with a royal blue tie, gray shorts, gray vest, gray blazer. On the crisp lapel of the scratchy blazer was the school crest, which featured the thin outline of a shield with an R and an S inside it. The R and the S were twined together like they were trying to strangle each other. In my dormitory, I put on my uniform, and then I went to class, where I sat counting the minutes until I could go home again.

The Ridge School was first established in 1919. The beautiful grounds sprawl out over nineteen acres on Westcliff Ridge, overlooking the upscale suburbs north of Johannesburg. The grand old buildings of stucco and stone are an excellent example of Cape Dutch architecture. There was a swimming pool and tennis courts, and stretched between stonewalled terraces, there was a big grassy field where boys played rugby and cricket. I sat across from the headmaster, who smiled at me over his huge desk and told me about the school's determination to grow high-achieving boys who think for themselves, speak their minds, excel at sport, and pass the matric with flying colors. (The matric is an exam you have to pass to graduate high school and get into college.) The Ridge offered grades one through seven, so age-wise, I was somewhere in the middle of the boarding school population. In its long, proud history, only a handful of black boys had attended the school. It was integrated just a few years before I was sent there, so I was in a vanishingly thin minority, and I quickly discovered that

I was even more isolated by my famous last name. I'm sure The Ridge School is a very fine school, but for me, it was intensely lonely, and I hated it. One Sunday evening at dinner, I told Madiba, "Granddad, I don't want to go back there."

"Ndaba, it's one of the finest preparatory schools in South Africa," he said. "Give it a bit more time. You'll get used to living there. You'll make friends."

"I have friends at *my* school."

"Is it possible to have too many friends?" He smiled and opened his hands in an expansive gesture. "Ndaba, you'll get the finest education. It's just a few years. Just through grade seven."

"Granddad, I hate it!" I struggled to explain it to him in English. In isiXhosa it would have sounded more manly, not like I was afraid or on the verge of tears. "Something gets broken—must be the black kid who broke it. Something goes missing—oh, must be that the black kid stole it."

Madiba sat quietly and took this in. His face settled into a frown.

My granddad had a way of listening that I have tried to emulate as an adult. He listened, motionless and focused, as if he was studying each word with a microscope. He didn't attempt to tell me that I was wrong or that my position was in some way irrelevant because I was a kid, and he didn't force me to return to The Ridge. He offered as a compromise that I should stay at home and attend Houghton Primary, where there were both boys and girls, and several black children, and I did try that for a while, but I missed my friends and cousins at Sacred Heart. I kept presenting my case—that Sacred Heart was only a few blocks farther for the driver to take me, that I would apply myself and get better grades, that I would work hard and gain his confidence—and eventually, Madiba relented.

Interesting thing about that "Bad" video: The extended version, a short film directed by Martin Scorsese, is actually the story of a black kid who goes to a mostly white boarding school and comes home to find that he has a difficult time connecting to his old crew. I returned to Sacred Heart, and my friends were glad to see me, but there was a subtle shift in things over the next few years. Even when I was back with my crew, my clique, I felt very much alone.

Aunt Makaziwe summed it up with a shrug. "You're a Mandela."

"My friends don't care about that," I said. These were the Gents, guys who'd known me most of my life.

"You'll know many people in your life," said Auntie Maki. "At my age, if one or two of them are real friends, you are very lucky."

I rolled my eyes. "I'm not a loser! I have at least a dozen friends."

"Mm-hmm." She just smiled and nodded. She didn't need me to know right then that she was right. She knew I would grow up and discover it for myself.

Having spent some time away, I had a whole new appreciation for my room, my Sega, and Mama Xoli's roasted chicken, salmon croquettes, and salted cod with potatoes. I suspect Mama Xoli was happy to have me back, as a great artist always enjoys seeing their work appreciated, and she never had to encourage me to eat. She and Mama Gloria had children of their own, and sometimes we all sat around the kitchen table together—a much noisier supper than the largely silent dinners I shared with Madiba. He was traveling a great deal, coping with the enormous issues that confronted him day after day.

Beyond the seemingly small matter of which song should be our national anthem, there was his standing on the stage of world politics. It may startle some Americans to know that the Old Man remained on the US government's terrorist watch list until 2008. Madiba's very first television interview happened in 1961, when he allowed Brian Widlake of ITN to meet him in a house where he was hiding from police. Widlake said,

"Do you see Africans being able to develop in this country without the Europeans being pushed out?"

"We have made it very clear in our policy," said Madiba, "that South Africa is a country of many races. There is room for all the various races in this country."

He stated then, very clearly, that the only goal of the ANC was democracy: one person, one vote. He never wavered from that stance and spoke out consistently in favor of peace and nonviolence, but he was arrested a year after this interview and sentenced to life in prison. Now he was in this position of power to do whatever he wanted, and it was difficult for people to accept that he was still advocating for people to be cool. I myself have a hard time with it, simply because I know I don't have it in me to spend three decades in prison and come out with a mouthful of forgiveness for the people who put me there. It seemed superhuman to me at the time, and while my understanding of the situation has evolved since then, my awe for him is still the same.

At the time of that 1961 interview, Madiba was only about five years older than I am now, and already he had that Madiba way of listening that I observed so much later in his life. He was as inscrutable as the Sphinx, but there is one moment—just a fraction of a second—when I detect a little side-eye. Check it out on YouTube.

You'll see what I'm saying. Widlake asks that question about Europeans being pushed out if Africans are "able to develop" in Africa, and in the split second between question and answer, it's like, *Really?* The question came, quite obviously, from a place of fear; Widlake was saying what everybody else was already thinking. But Africans had "developed" the continent for thousands of years before the Europeans came. The Africans had a rich culture, strong social and familial bonds, and a wealth of natural resources before Europeans came in, appropriated the land, and spread diseases. (Is any of this sounding vaguely familiar, America?)

So the suggestion of Europeans getting "pushed out" and Africans being "allowed to develop" was beyond ironic. Madiba could have gone off on that, and as I mentioned before, he could scold proper. He could shut a person down. His extraordinary superpower was that he chose not to. In that moment and a million other moments when he found himself sitting across from somebody who just didn't get it, he chose to go forward instead of back. He chose to find common ground rather than refight a battle his ancestors had already lost. He talked about the possibility of peace instead of the go-nowhere cycle of conflict. I wonder how the overall tone of the Internet would shift if more people were able to shut off their need to be right about everything at any given moment. What would happen if the desire to do right won out over the desire to prove somebody else wrong?

Madiba loved to repeat The Story of the Lady on the Phone: During the campaign, before he was elected president, he was trying to get some business done and placed a call.

He asks the lady who answered the phone, "To whom am I speaking?"

She gets feisty and answers, "You're speaking to *me*."

He politely asks her name, but she gets cross. "Who are you to ask my name? What's *your* name?"

"Well, tell me your name and then I'll tell you mine," he says, and they start going back and forth. She doesn't get that he's being humble, trying to spare her some embarrassment, so she says, "You seem like a very backward person. Have you even passed your matric?"

He says, "Be careful. If the qualification to speak to you is to possess a matric certificate, I might work hard to pass my matric and be in the same class you are."

This was unthinkable to the lady. She says, "You'll never be in the same class as me." And she hangs up on him.

Madiba always ended the story with a sly smile. "How I wish she were here today!"

The story always got a big laugh, but I don't think

that's the only reason he told it. He never pointed out that if this lady had thought she was talking to another white person, she wouldn't have treated him that way. In fact, he never specifically said that she was white. It's not a story about her being white; it's a story about her being prejudiced. It's about how assumptions based on prejudice make us look profoundly foolish. Perhaps there would have been some small satisfaction in telling her his name and making her feel small, but certainly not so great as the satisfaction he got from telling that story and hearing people laugh at the sheer stupidity of blind racism.

Arriving home at the end of a trip abroad, the Old Man always came to my room, even if it was a little past my strict ten o'clock curfew. I was always glad to hear his footsteps in the hallway. I didn't run to him and throw my arms around him. The thought never even crossed my mind. We greeted each other with a handshake, dignified and manly. He was very weary most evenings, so I didn't try to engage him in a long conversation. I knew he'd be up early, and if I got up early too, we would work out together.

Madiba was religious about his morning walk, and the rest of his daily exercise routine was usually some combination of skipping rope, press-ups, and weights. He introduced me to the medicine ball and took me through his favorite moves with it. "Lunge like so. Good. And now press it up. Up, up! Straight up! That's it. Very good. To the side now. Keep it up here, Ndaba, at the level of your shoulder." Looking back, I cherish those early morning hours with my granddad, though I had a hard time keeping up with him. He was almost eighty years old, but he'd always been fastidious about taking care of himself and staying healthy, even while he was in prison.

"On the Island" he said, "when there was talk about a hunger strike, I said, 'Why should we, who are already fighting for our lives, punish ourselves with deprivation?' No, no. We had to eat whatever meat and vegetables were available to us. We had to take care of ourselves, keep ourselves strong enough to resist. Better to punish them with slow-downs and refusing to do the work."

The bleakness of his life in prison was a stark contrast to the beauty of his life in Qunu. As we lunged and lifted and twisted with our medicine balls, he told me about how he used to climb up on the back of an elderly bull and ride around the fields near his mother's hut.

"We'll go there someday, Ndaba. I'll show you where your Old Man comes from," he said. "You'd like to go there, wouldn't you?"

"Yes, Granddad." I was breathing hard, thinking about what it would be like to ride on a bull.

"I was born in Mvezo, where my father was chief, but Qunu is where I was happiest when I was a boy. Of course, I had to obey my father, and we all acted according to the customs of the tribe, but other than that, I was free to do as I pleased. You were born fighting to be free, Ndaba, but you'll grow up and live free. I was born free—swimming, running, going wherever I wanted to go, doing whatever I wanted to do—and then I grew up. I became a man and went out into the world and discovered that this freedom I enjoyed as a child—it was an illusion."

We'd stay at it until I felt like my arms were going to fall off, and then he'd clap my shoulder and say, "Keep working on it!" before he sent me to shower and get ready for school, and I'd go about my day, not thinking all that much about everything he'd said, not realizing how those stories were working their way into my slowly awakening awareness of the world around me, which is another way to say "political consciousness," I suppose. I was politically aware from a very young age. I knew what apartheid was, and I knew we had to fight it, but so much of my understanding was limited to "black versus white."

Madiba wrote in *Long Walk to Freedom*: "Freedom is indivisible.... [T]he oppressor must be liberated just as surely as the oppressed. A man who takes away another man's freedom is a prisoner of hatred, he is locked behind the bars of prejudice....The oppressed and the oppressor alike are robbed of their humanity."

This is the root of Madiba's compassion for the white people of South Africa, as inconceivable as that was for many of his comrades in the struggle for liberation. To hate them would have meant exchanging one prison for another. So he celebrated the Springboks' victory with them, and he let them keep that stolid march as the national anthem for a little while, and then he very patiently, through proper channels and committees and process, evolved a new anthem that combined "Die Stem van Suid-Afrika" with an old hymn, "Nkosi Sikelel' iAfrika" ("Lord Bless Africa").

Albertina Sisulu was in the courtroom at the end of the Rivonia Trial in 1963, when Madiba and six ANC colleagues, including Walter Sisulu, were sentenced to life in prison. She wasn't allowed to speak to her husband, but she ran outside to catch what might be her last glimpse of him and Madiba and the others, who were like family to her. As they were taken away, Albertina and other members of the ANC Women's League formed an honor guard in Pretoria's Church Square. When I was a kid, I couldn't hear "Nkosi Sikelel' iAfrika" without hearing their hearts breaking. There's a mournful quality in the melody at first, but then it soars to the chorus, full of faith in this future that was a long time coming, but did arrive in Albertina's lifetime. Because she and others like her made it happen. They didn't sit around waiting for God to do it. Their faith in this future was an unshakable faith in themselves.

The words in isiXhosa:

Nkosi sikelel' iAfrika
Maluphakanyisw' uhondo lwayo

In Afrikaans:

Hou u hand, o Heer, oor Afrika
Lei ons tot by eenheid en begrip

In English:

Lord, bless Africa
May her spirit rise high up

Madiba sang it with great gusto in any language, and now I understand why he wanted me to be comfortable in all three languages as well. Elegant isiXhosa is where I come from. Afrikaans set me on a level playing field with my white countrymen. English opened a doorway to the rest of our continent and the world beyond it.

5

Uzawubona uba umoya ubheka ngaphi.

"Listen to the direction of the wind."

Like millions of other kids my age, I could flaw-lessly rap the entire theme song of *The Fresh Prince of Bel-Air*, which sets up the premise of this show about a black kid from the projects and how his life "got flipped" by sheer good fortune of family ties. He's whisked by car from a big city slum to the posh suburbs where he is a super cool fish out of water and decides he "might as well kick it." It was impossible to ignore the similarity to my circumstances. What was remarkable about this show, though I didn't think of it this way at the time, was the juxtaposition of mentor and mentee. The benefits to the kid were obvious; you don't need DJ Jazzy Jeff to spell it out for you. Instead, the focus was on how the boy improved the life and opened the mind of the rich uncle.

My granddad was keenly aware of how much he'd missed, sitting in prison for twenty-seven years, and he looked forward to reconnecting—or connecting for the first time—with the younger generations in his family. When he came out of jail, all he wanted to do was return to his family and continue his work with the ANC. He stayed briefly with his friend Desmond Tutu, and then went home to Qunu, because "a man should have a home within sight of the place he was born." He had a house built almost identical to the one he was staying in the first time I met him, the warden's house at Victor Verster Prison. I wasn't the only one who thought this was a very strange thing to do, but the Old Man played it off with a shrug.

"I was used to that place," he said. "I didn't want to wander around in the night looking for the kitchen."

I think his intention was to live quietly, write books, speak widely, and remain influential as a private citizen.

When it was proposed that he should stand as the ANC candidate for president in South Africa's first democratic election, he was not in favor of this idea. He strongly stated that the candidate should be a younger person, a man or woman who'd been living in the culture, not separate from it, and who understood the emerging technologies that were changing everything about the world.

In the run-up to the election, there was hardcore violence between followers of the Inkatha Freedom Party, who were mostly Zulu, and the ANC, in which the leadership (at that time) was mostly Xhosa but whose membership was more diverse than any other party. It served the purposes of the white government to have these factions hack on each other with machetes, because that made it look like black people could never come together in a civilized manner to govern their own country. Much publicity was given to the barbaric practice of "necklacing"—placing a petrol-filled tire around a person and setting it on fire—and to outrageous incidents of street violence, during which white police often stood by and watched.

Madiba pleaded for peace, and it became increasingly obvious that he was the only one capable of bringing people together and leading the country toward something that resembled unity. His separation from society all those years had left him with that "thirty-thousand-foot view" a leader aspires to, a perspective that took in the big picture without the distraction of past day-to-day issues. Nonetheless, once he was in office, he knew he still needed that youthful perspective, and I think I was part of that, but the major infusion of *Fresh Prince* at the house in Houghton came from my older brother Mandla.

Mandla's mother was my father's first wife. They divorced when my brother was little, and she took him to live in London long before our dad met and married my mom.

I'd been living with the Old Man for a little over a year when my brother Mandla arrived, and I've never been so glad to see anyone in my life. As president, my granddad traveled a lot and worked long, hard hours seven days a week. Everyone in the house was good to me, but it was pretty lonely sometimes. Mandla was a link to my dad at a time when my dad seemed very far away. Having grown up with his mother in London, Mandla was worldly and confident. For a while, he went to Waterford Kamhlaba, a Swaziland prep school Auntie Zindzi and Auntie Zenani had also attended back in the day. Now he was coming and going from university, showing little more interest in his classes than I was able to muster for grade seven.

I worshipped Mandla. In my mind, he was the coolest of the cool. He was my idol. I had just turned thirteen, and Mandla was nine years older than me, so he had already experienced "going to the mountain" and was living the big life of a twenty-something, frequenting clubs, romancing women, and driving a nice car. He was every bit as tall as the Old Man, but he had a stockier build, more like Madiba as a young man, before prison left him lean and self-disciplined. This was 1996, the grunge moment for music and fashion in Europe and the United States, but Mandla was way ahead of that curve. He cut straight from the jewel-tone pleather of the 1980s to full hip-hop with the sideways baseball cap and Ice Cube bomber jacket.

Mandla was an aspiring DJ, so he had an epic collection of CDs and an encyclopedic knowledge of hip-hop and rap music from around the world. I was used to coming home to the silent house and heading for the kitchen where Auntie Xoli listened to choral gospel music—and don't get me wrong, South African choral music is amazing—but I loved opening the door and hearing the pounding bass emanating from Mandla's room down the hall from mine. I quickly became a hip-hop head. Whatever he was listening to, that's what I wanted to know everything about, and at the time, that was all hip-hop and rap and maybe five percent reggae.

Before that, my friends and I were into kwaito, a form of house music that smashed up big basslines, percussion loops, and traditional African vocals through a deft use of new editing technology. It was like our version of hip-hop before hip-hop really became a thing in South Africa. Kwaito was born in the ghettos of Johannesburg in the early 1990s and gets its name from the Afrikaans word *kwaai*, which means "angry," and from *Amakwaito*, old school gangsters from the 1950s. It sampled equally from African music of the previous seven decades, all the way back to the scratchy recordings of the 1920s, and from current British and American club music. Madiba was down with the kwaito. You'd catch him doing this particular dance move—small back and forth steps, elbows swinging at a ninety-degree angle—that came to be known as "the Madiba shuffle." In many ways, kwaito embodied that desire he had expressed to make way for youthful voices, hopefully bringing the spirit and traditions of African culture into the present. He didn't know how to send an email, but he sensed that a technological revolution was coming, and he wanted South Africa to be part of it.

Me, I just thought it was dope. Reggae music, on the other hand, sparked a whole new awareness about politics and the history of resistance all over the world. Burning Spear's *Marcus Garvey* album introduced me to the Jamaican founder of Pan-Africanism. Tappa Zukie sang about Stephen Biko, who led and died for the Black Consciousness Movement in South Africa. I started asking questions, and the Old Man was glad to talk about people and issues I was learning about from Bob Marley and Lee "Scratch" Perry.

"Granddad, I heard a song about Robert Sobukwe. It had Robben Island in it."

"Yes," said the Old Man. "He was there when I was there, but they kept him in solitary confinement most of the time. He was a teacher. Deep thinker. Brilliant orator. He knew how to bring an idea to life. And ideas, you know?" He tapped his finger against his temple. "Ideas were considered very dangerous. I didn't agree with everything he said, but I was very keen to talk with him. They let us speak to each other at first, but then they decided, 'Those two heads together—Mandela and Sobukwe—that could spell trouble.' They put us in cells at opposite ends of the corridor. When his three-year sentence had been served, they came up with a new rule, The Sobukwe Clause, making it possible to hold a political prisoner indefinitely without even presenting charges against him. So he was there another six years. In 1969, the warden started a daily news broadcast for the prisoners. Naturally, all the news was about how things were going so well for the government and so badly for anyone who opposed them. The very first broadcast began with the announcement of the death of Robert Sobukwe. So now they sing a song about him. That's good."

When Mandla came along and took all this to the next level with rap and hip-hop, it blew my mind. Kwaito had a political edge, but it was mostly about pride, joy, and a freedom of spirit that couldn't be snuffed out by the oppression of apartheid. This stuff Mandla was listening to was straight out of Compton by way of Liverpool, full of outrage and revolution. There was this attitude of aggression, this energy that made you proud to be black, proud of coming from where you were coming from. Hip-hop at that time had a conscious message about socioeconomic conditions and challenges, about the incredibly harsh realities faced by the people of that moment. It was powerful because it awakened political consciousness and gave it a voice. It demanded respect. "You had to insist on respect from day one," Madiba said about his early years on Robben Island, and there was a similar dynamic in hip-hop back then. It was like, "Yeah, we know who you think you are, but *this* is who we are." It raised us up in our own self-respect and elevated our standing with our peers. It was no longer possible to ignore this voice or the troubled place it came from.

The dinner table was a lot less quiet with Mandla

around. Because he had experienced going to the mountain, he and the Old Man conversed man to man. Madiba and I had grown closer, but the way they talked to each other was on a different level. I was old enough to pick up on that and feel a pang of envy. I wasn't all that excited about the idea of going to the mountain, but I thought it would be cool to be an equal part of those conversations about politics and current events and even about girls. I was intensely interested in all of these topics, but was still considering how best to engage with these interests and translate that into action—particularly the girls. I was a bit of a late bloomer in that area. History was the subject that interested me the most, but I hadn't quite started connecting the dots between history and current world politics or between world politics and current cultural trends. Mandla, on the other hand, had strong ideas about politics, was quite in the know on the cultural watershed, and considered himself very smooth with the ladies.

Not long after he came to live with Madiba and me, Mandla decided to go to Hong Kong to visit his mom, and he suggested that I should be allowed to go with him. This was, quite simply, the most thrilling thing anyone could have possibly suggested. Waiting for the Old Man's answer, I was afraid to breathe. He listened to Mandla's pitch about how educational it would be and then nodded.

"Yes, I think that would be a very good experience. It's good for young people to broaden their horizons," he said, and Mandla and I agreed with this quite enthusiastically, but I think the definition of "good experience" was different in all three of our minds.

We got to Hong Kong, and Mandla showed me the city. He was super cool with it all. Having been there before, he knew his way around. He decided we should hit a few clubs one night, but as we arrived at the first place, I was getting very nervous. I was tall for my age, but I was only thirteen.

"How am I going to get in?" I asked Mandla.

"Just walk in," he said, and before I could object, he walked past the bouncer and through the door. I started to follow him, but I had hesitated just long enough to arouse the bouncer's suspicion.

"Hold up, mate." He extended his beefy arm between me and the entrance. "How old are you?"

I was like, "Uhhhhhh . . . eighteen?"

He huffed and shook his head. "Not today, bro."

Mandla checked over his shoulder to make sure I was with him, and when he saw that I wasn't, he rolled his eyes and came back out. We were on a brightly lit strip with one club after another, so we moved along to the next one.

"Come on, man," he said. "You have to have confidence. Just walk on in there."

As we approached the door, I walked as tall as I could, pacing my steps to match Mandla's, trying to carry my skinny shoulders with the same authoritative posture he had. He sauntered past the bouncer, and I sauntered along in his shadow. The gatekeeper didn't say a word, and I purposely didn't look him in the eye. I don't know if he took me for an eighteen-year-old or just decided to let it slide. Either way, we sailed right in the door and over to the bar. It was pretty cool. The music was great, the girls were beautiful, and I ended up having a long, interesting conversation with a couple of Americans who were stationed at a military base near Hong Kong. By the time we returned home to Johannesburg, my horizons had definitely been widened.

"You should go see your mom," Mandla said after we returned home to Houghton. I wasn't sure this was a good idea, but seeing Mandla with his mom did make me wonder how it might work out.

"I don't know where she lives," I said.

"The Old Man got her a house in the East Rand," said Mandla. "She had a baby, you know."

"What?" I was stunned to hear it.

"Oh, yes. We have another brother," said Mandla.

"His name is Andile. He's a cute little bugger. Tell the Old Man you want to go see them."

I thought about it a while before I finally worked up the courage to ask my granddad. No one ever said it wasn't okay to mention my mom. No one ever said anything against her. It was just a vibe that had been in the air from the beginning. Like I knew there was a lot I didn't know. When I finally did ask the Old Man, he sighed heavily and looked genuinely sad.

"She left the house I provided her in the East Rand," he said. "She left the job that was provided for her. She went home to her family in Soweto. Her auntie is caring for the baby."

"Can Bhut drive me?"

He considered it, looking at me as if he noticed just that minute how much taller I had gotten since I arrived.

"Yes," he said. "You should go."

So I went. I wish I could say that it was great, but it wasn't. I was happy to see my mom, and she kept telling me how proud of me she was, but she was a feisty lady, and after a drink or two, she got pretty sassy to everyone around her. "What a tall, handsome son I have! Oh, yes, I have a son." She and my father were completely over, she said, and she was seeing some guy. She wanted me to meet him. She dragged me to his house and pounded on the door. "That's right! I have a son!"

I'll be honest. It sucked. It was weird. I was scared. The last thing I wanted was for some strange, hulking dude to open that door. Luckily, he wasn't home, and before too much longer, Bhut came to drive me home.

I didn't see or hear from my mom for a long time. During high school I saw her maybe once or twice a year. I was glad to see her, but I was always happy to get home to Mama Xoli, who was truly—if we're being totally honest—the primary mother figure in my life. I'm not sure she'll ever know what she has meant to me.

When I told Mandla about my visit to Soweto, he said, "We need to bring Mbuso and Andile home with us."

Our granddad was not super in favor of this idea. He loved these little guys—he loved all his grandchildren and great-grandchildren—but Mbuso was only five years old and Andile was a baby, so this was asking Mama Xoli and Mama Gloria to step up their commitment to a whole different level, well beyond the relatively low maintenance we older kids required. Mandla was adamant: "We're brothers. We should be together."

It took a while to win the Old Man over, but about a year after Mandla arrived, Mbuso came to live with us, and a year or so later, two-year-old Andile joined us as well. For the most part, Mama Xoli and Mama Gloria and the other ladies who worked in the house cared for the little ones, but Mandla let me know it was my turn to step up as big brother, and I loved that role. Andile and Mbuso were my connection to my mom, and I think having all four of us together at the noisy dinner table made our granddad feel a bit more connected to my dad and the family that had been taken from him.

M ADIBA HAD MADE A statement to the press in 1992 that he and Mama Winnie had separated, but they weren't actually divorced until 1996. He said very little about this in his own writing and speaking. The Old Man was circumspect about addressing personal issues and determined to protect the privacy of his family. His books were about politics and history, and he was humble about his place in it. He liked to speak about Qunu, the place where he'd spent his childhood, and was happy to talk about that during interviews, but when questions turned to personal or family matters, he'd sit with a stony smile and shake his head, consistently polite but quite immovable.

"Mr. Mandela, now that your divorce has become final—"

"I have said I won't be dealing with personal issues."

"Mr. Mandela, your relationship with Graça Machel, the former First Lady of Mozambique—"

"I'm not answering that."

"Ah. I see. All right then. What about Mrs. Machel's—"

"Please remind your editor I have said I won't be dealing with personal issues."

Graça Machel was widowed in 1986 when her husband, Samora Machel, the president of Mozambique was killed in a plane crash. She was a formidable woman with her own history of resisting colonialism in her country. She was gracious and diplomatic, but I read somewhere that she could take an assault rifle apart and put it back together in a matter of minutes. She was uniquely suited to share Madiba's complicated life. Years later, in a conversation with the BBC, she described it as a "very mature" relationship between "two people who had been very hurt by life."

She said, "After he lost the biggest love of his life— which is Winnie—he believed, *It's over.* He's not young anymore. He thought he'd concentrate on his political life and children and grandchildren." Graça was still involved in politics, an international advocate for the rights of women and children, so she and Madiba were acquaintances, and then friends, and then confidants. By the time Mandla came to live with us, we had begun teasing the Old Man about having a girlfriend. Eventually, a spokesman for the family made a subdued statement to the press: "I've been authorized to confirm that there is a close relationship—or friendship—that exists between the president and Mrs. Graça Machel. It's been going on for a while, and the president is comfortable in it."

Madiba and Graça were married on his eightieth birthday in a small ceremony with only our family and a few friends attending. There was a complicated plot to keep the press distracted, which wasn't all that difficult, because the wedding was one of the few quiet moments in a huge blur of birthday festivities. The celebration started Thursday afternoon at Kruger National Park, where the Old Man joined a thousand orphans who were served a 260-pound birthday cake. On Sunday, there was a gigantic gala to raise money for Madiba's favorite charities through his Millennium Fund. Celebrity guests included Stevie Wonder, Danny Glover, and Michael Jackson.

The arrival of the reigning King of Pop was more than enough to distract the attention of the press, and in the mind of every kid in our family, it was a much bigger deal than two old folks finally getting married. The whole family gathered in a room at a friend's house in Johannesburg where Michael was staying. The little kids were on the sofa with Madiba, practically bouncing out of their shorts. I stood back a bit with Mandla and our cousin Kweku and the other older kids, doing our best to remain nonchalant. We couldn't believe how lucky we were to be hanging out, singing happy birth-day, and eating cake with Michael Jackson. When I look at the video of that moment, I see Mandla and me in the midst of it all, meticulously casual and purposely cool.

During those years, I learned a lot from Mandla, the Fresh Prince who made us all laugh and dogged us when we didn't do right. I have to give him credit for the way he stepped up as the older brother. He included me in his life, shared his music with me, and took time to edu-cate me on the fundamentals of how to be a guy. It's a bit painful to think about, if I'm honest, because Mandla and I are not close now. Logistically, if one brother was in need, the other could be at his side in a couple of hours, but in all the ways that matter—ideologically, personally, emotionally—we are worlds apart. I did the worst thing a little brother can do: I grew up. And Mandla did the worst thing an older brother can do: He disappointed me.

If you have brothers or sisters, you already know how and why adult siblings become estranged from each other, especially when the patriarchs and matriarchs are fading or gone. Given the position we Mandelas find ourselves in, those dynamics are taken to the tenth power in my family, so the circumstances are unique, but I assure you, the actual family dynamic is no differ-ent from yours.

We all make choices in our lives that are maybe not the choices our siblings would make. Someone wants something. Someone has something. Someone does something. Someone says something. In the moment, the issue always seems extremely important. As time goes by, grudges become deeply entrenched, and the time always goes by much faster than you would have believed possible. You're left with a sad state of questioning: Is reconciliation possible? Is it worth it? Will it take too much of my pride or cost too much of my brother's dignity? Reconciliation—in a family, in a country, in a person's own heart—is a complicated process. Forgiveness is not for the faint of heart. Sometimes it takes a strong stomach.

In April 1996, mandated by the Promotion of National Unity and Reconciliation Act, South Africa's Truth and Reconciliation Commission (TRC) headed by Archbishop Desmond Tutu began formal hearings in Cape Town. Over the next two years, with many sessions airing on national TV and radio, the hearings opened the floor to victims of violence and other abuses under apartheid (from 1960 to 1994). The goal was to restore the dignity of those who'd been violated, to facilitate rehabilitation and reparation if possible, and in some cases, to grant amnesty to those willing to come forward and accept responsibility for things they'd done wrong.

This was a huge undertaking, and it was a bitter moment for everyone in South Africa, but it was a compassionate, cleansing endeavor, the beginning of reality-based healing, as opposed to the fairy tale of the rugby match that magically made us all brothers. Racism is a cultural cancer, and the TRC was South Africa's first round of chemotherapy: painful, sickening, and necessary. We still have a lot of work to do, but I believe, thanks to Madiba, we're light years ahead of the powerful nations who live in deep denial of the malignant racism infecting their culture. Madiba created an imperfect but progressive structure in which forgiveness was possible, and people responded to it, partly because they knew he shared the deep personal cost of accountability.

One of the people who stood before the TRC's Human Rights Violations Committee in 1997 was Mama Winnie, and she was not testifying as a victim; she stood as the accused. The committee had already heard testimony implicating the Mandela United Football Club, a soccer team that functioned as Mama Winnie's bodyguards, in several murders and assaults during the violent death throes of apartheid. In 1986, four years before Madiba was released from prison, Mama Winnie stood before a crowd who'd gathered to hear her in Munsieville and made an impassioned speech about the evils of apartheid, about injustice and intolerable cruelty, and in the heat of that moment, she said, "Together, hand in hand, with our boxes of matches and our necklaces, we shall liberate this country!" The crowd went wild. The media went nuts. The ANC went into panic mode. Necklacing was a terrifying practice that inevitably led to the buzzword "savage" being applied to black South Africans in the media. It should not be mentioned lightly and can not be condoned. But this was Mama Winnie. People loved her. With all she'd done and suffered in the course of this fight, the ANC couldn't distance themselves from her.

Years after all of this crazy, regrettable, inconceivable shit went down, Mama Winnie sat before the TRC and spoke with dignity and sadness about the terrible events of those years, during which she'd been deeply wronged, imprisoned, tortured, and kept in solitary confinement. Urged by Tutu, she conceded that she had wronged others as well and that toward the end, things had "gone horribly wrong," particularly in the beating death of a fourteen-year-old boy. She apologized to the families of the victims. I don't know what, if any, apology was offered to her.

It broke Madiba's heart. He loved this remarkable woman and knew how greatly she had suffered. There was a great deal of stress in the family and in the ANC over this, and sometimes I hated hearing the harsh sound of those voices I loved. I wanted to go back to the laughing and loud music. I wanted everyone to love everyone else, and I didn't want my little brothers to grow up with the kind of violence and strife I'd witnessed at that age. It was a hard thing to get past, but Madiba, for the most part was stoic about it. He said nothing to me about the hearings, and I didn't ask, but there was a noticeable weight of sadness on him some days. He and Mama Winnie weren't together, and they disagreed strongly on a lot of things, but it was clear that their love and respect for each other never faltered.

In 2001, there was an odd incident at a Youth Day event commemorating the twenty-fifth anniversary of the Soweto uprising. Mama Winnie arrived late and was slow getting to the podium because of the crowd gathered to greet her. When she went to greet Thabo Mbeki, then president of South Africa, with a kiss on the cheek, he brushed her aside aggressively enough to knock her baseball cap off her head. She wasn't hurt, but it looked very bad. The media went insane, because that's what they do. The more surprising thing was how angry Madiba got when he saw the videotape of the awkward moment.

"How could he do such a thing?" The Old Man wagged his finger at the TV. "That is no way to treat a woman. Any woman. But a grandmother? A colleague who's made unimaginable sacrifices for the cause of freedom? No! It is not acceptable."

Mbeki tried to call him that evening, but when the secretary brought the telephone to the dining room, Madiba said, "Take it away. I'm not taking his calls." He wanted Mandla and I to learn from this that there was never an excuse to hit or manhandle a woman. No matter the circumstances, that was a line that must not be crossed. The Old Man thought highly of Mbeki in general, however, and he was all about reconciliation. I don't know what passed between them or how Mbeki found his way back to Madiba's good graces, but my granddad never made people kowtow to him. He didn't hide his disappointment or irritation, but he wanted people to rise above their worst moments and redeem themselves, particularly if the person was family or a friend.

Perhaps in some ways, it's easier to make peace with a stranger than it is to make peace with a good friend or even a brother. A stranger doesn't share so much history, not so much water under the bridge. Between brothers, there's vulnerability, a greater potential to wound and be wounded. So we try to swallow our anger, and we hope others will swallow their anger at us. Forgive and forget, right?

But this is something else I learned from my grandfather: Anger has its place, even in a kind heart. Anger is an essential part of forgiveness, because denying our anger holds forgiveness at arm's length and prevents us from rising above it.

Madiba asked his black countrymen to forgive, but he never asked them to forget. He made sure that the wrongs perpetrated during apartheid became part of our written and recorded history—even those wrongs committed by people who were dear to him, the very people who were fighting for his freedom. Speaking only for myself, there's no way in hell I would be able to come out of prison after almost three decades and tell my family to throw their guns in the ocean. There are no words for that in the lexicon of ordinary people. We needed Madiba to plow that path for us to follow, and he did that at great personal cost, his focus firmly fixed on the greater good.

"For me," Madiba said, "nonviolence was not a moral principal but a strategy."

Uzawubona uba umoya ubheka ngaphi, the old saying goes. "Listen to the direction of the wind." The Old Man sat in prison all those years, and he listened. He observed what was happening all around us in Uganda, Zimbabwe, and Nigeria. They gained their independence and immediately kicked the white people out. In the Congo, all the white and Indian people were ordered to leave. Suddenly, the economy's dead—and it stays

dead for a long time. Nothing moves. With their enemies gone, the people turn on each other, drawing new
lines of hatred based on religion or ideology or fear—
anything that can be skillfully used by those who seek
to control a populace, those who understand that people
are a lot easier to control when they're splintered instead
of united. Poverty and desperation allow the worst sort
of authoritarianism to arise, whether that be dictators
like Idi Amin or a conman who scams his way into a
presidency or any one of a thousand petty bureaucrats
who've been bullied all their lives and are hungry for a
taste of power over others.

Madiba was determined that this would not happen
in South Africa. He believed we were capable of more
than chaos and vengeance, and he had ten thousand
days to think about how that might work. He formed
a strategy, and key to it was the unshakable stance that
we must move forward together—many races, one
country—but he didn't ask people to forgive as a favor
to those who'd wronged them; he asked them to do it for
themselves and their children.

"In that day," Grandma Evelyn used to read from the
Old Testament, "the wolf will live with the lamb, the leop-
ard will lie down with the goat, the calf and the lion and
the yearling together; and a little child will lead them."

This passage paints a beautiful picture of a peaceful

world, but it doesn't come with an instruction manual. Madiba provided a blueprint. He established a new paradigm for forgiveness that could only be explained as a gift from God, but I see now that the gift wasn't some saintly ability to forgive and forget. God's gift to Madiba was the wisdom to understand forgiveness as part of a leadership strategy. As an economic principle. As a key component to reconciliation, which is the only true way forward for any society or any family. Another key component is justice, and you can't find that looking back, only looking forward.

Under the Restitution of Land Rights Act of 1994, the government bought land from white owners and restored it to black people who'd farmed it for generations before apartheid. In 1998, Madiba went to KwaZulu-Natal for a ceremony where eighty-five black families received 600,000 hectares. He said, "Our land reform program helps redress the injustices of apartheid. It fosters national reconciliation and stability." Meanwhile, the president of Zimbabwe had just laid down notice that white owners were going to be sent packing without compensation. His vibe was, "I'm not going to buy my own Rolex from the pickpocket who stole it." Some people thought Madiba should get rough and expel the whites, but he pushed for patience and peace. Twenty years on, both are getting hard to maintain. There is a

compassionate, equitable way to structure land redistribution, and when we find that working business model,
we will have found the key to forging peace and equality
on a global scale, but it hasn't happened yet.

In 2018, World Bank's Gini Index, a standard tool
that measures economic inequality, ranked South Africa
dead last of 149 countries studied. Dead. Last. The
recent report says the top 1 percent of South Africans
(predominantly white) own 70.9 percent of the nation's
wealth. The bottom 60 percent (predominantly black)
own about 7 percent. It's an obvious artifact of colonialism and apartheid. My black brothers and sisters
can't sit in bitterness or pretend that it relieves them of
responsibility for their own lives, but my white brothers
and sisters can't deny that they still enjoy the benefits of
apartheid. There has to come a time when we children
of apartheid, black and white, say to each other, "Look,
my grandparents were not right with your grandparents.
My parents were not right with your parents. But I want
to be right with you." We have to be the generation who
understands that racism, sexism, homophobia, religious
bigotry—inequality in all its ugly guises—splinters the
most powerful asset available to humankind: unity.

6

Ulwazi alukhulelwa.

"One does not become great by claiming greatness."

Among the old stories the Old Man loved to tell were several that involved a hare outwitting bullies far bigger and physically stronger than himself.

"You must think like the hare," said Madiba. "That hare was a trickster." And then he'd launch into one of Hare's many exploits, like the time Buffalo invites Hare to accompany him on a long journey. Since Buffalo can intimidate all the other animals into doing whatever he wants, Hare thinks this is the side to be on, until Buffalo says, "Since I'm letting you hang with me, Hare, I expect you to carry my sleeping mat." And he piles this heavy bedroll on poor Hare's back. They travel for a day or two, and Hare is really over this sleeping mat thing, but he's afraid to say anything to Buffalo, who could step on him and end any argument right there. So he says, "Buffalo, you must be hungry. You go ahead, and since I'm a lot faster, I'll dash into these woods and pick some fruit for you and catch up later." Buffalo knows Hare would not dare try to run off, so he agrees and goes down the road. Hare darts into the woods and picks a few apples, but he's really looking for a honey tree, and he finds one. He rolls out Buffalo's sleeping mat, uses a long stick to spread it with honey, lets the bees swarm onto it, and rolls it up again. He and Buffalo get to their destination, and Buffalo goes into a hut where they're supposed to stay, and Buffalo is like, "No, you sleep outside. This is my hut." And Hare's like, "No worries. I'll lock the door after you go in so nobody bothers you. Don't forget your bedroll."

You can guess what happens when Buffalo unrolls the sleeping mat full of bees. Madiba's depiction of the big bully in a subsequent world of hurt made us laugh our heads off. His storytelling skills improved with the arrival of Mbuso and Andile, because they were still little enough to believe in magic rivers and talking trees. He loved to make them laugh with silly voices and big gestures. The Old Man had softened somewhat since my arrival, and honestly, those two were quite spoiled. Rigid discipline was still very much the rule for me, but all that seemed to fly out the window when it came to Mbuso and Andile. He seemed to click to the idea that there was more pleasure in storytelling than there was in policing an immaculately clean room.

Mbuso and Andile were "born frees": children who had no memory of apartheid. Madiba liked the idea of this new generation learning about apartheid in school someday, scratching their heads and saying, "That is *whack!*"—or whatever they would be saying in that era. During this era, because we watched a lot of *In Living Color* in the late 1990s, the expression was usually, "I don't think so!" or "Homey don't play dat," and then you'd wallop the other person with a sofa pillow.

But back to Buffalo and Hare.

"You see, it's about strategy," said the Old Man. "Like boxing. On the battlefield, Buffalo wins, because he has the brute strength. In the boxing ring, Hare has a chance, because boxing is science. Boxing is an art form. It's physics and geometry."

Madiba and I watched the first Tyson-Holyfield "Finally" fight in 1996. It was the middle of the night, so I was bleary-eyed but excited to be out of bed and in on the action. The fight raged on to a much-contested finish, with Holyfield retaining his title and Tyson complaining bitterly about head-butting the ref had declared accidental. The rematch in June 1997 was sold on pay-per-view as "The Sound and the Fury," and there was plenty of both. It was a major event at our house.

"Ndaba, wake up." Mandla came into my room and rousted me out in the middle of the night. "Come down to the lounge. It's starting soon."

The match began at 6:00 PM on a Saturday night in Las Vegas, which made it stupid o'clock Sunday morning in Johannesburg. I think it was about 3:00 AM. As a general rule, the Old Man was early to bed, early to rise, and I still had a 10:00 PM curfew (in theory, although there was seldom anyone actually policing it), but he was not going to miss this fight and neither was I. Mandla and I posted up in the lounge with the Old Man, eating Provita with Beefy Bovril (way better than Vegemite), waiting for the big event to begin, and listening to our granddad wax philosophical about the egalitarian nature of boxing. He appreciated any moment when race, social status, and money fell away, leaving only the true nature of a person.

"In the ring, you're thinking only about strategy," he said. "How to protect yourself. How to best your opponent. You circle each other, probing strengths and weaknesses. Not just the physical, but what is in this man's eyes."

Madiba's love of boxing is well documented. He was good at it when he was young, and while he was watching the prefight show, he couldn't help adopting a sort of punchy posture in his wingback chair, with fists balled up and elbows tucked in tight against his ribcage.

"In the ring, you see a man's true character," he said. "The very first time I went to the US, I met Holyfield. I met the champ. Many Americans offered words of support. He was one of those who knew that words are not enough. We needed resources for the cause of freedom to win."

Round One commenced. Holyfield and Tyson went at each other, and it looked like it was going to be a long, brutal fight. Round Two was paused over an accidental head-butt that left Tyson with blood streaming down from a cut over his eye.

"Tyson is being bullied in there," the announcer said. "Holyfield is really taking the fight to him."

"Yes, yes!" Madiba was on his feet now. "This is where they summon an amazing will. When they start to feel the pain."

The bell clanged. Two rounds gone, and it looked like Holyfield was going to beat the living crap out of Tyson. But in Round Three, Tyson came hammering back. The dialogue from Mandla and me mainly consisted of "Oh. OH! *Whooaaah*," and so forth. The Old Man seemed to have a running conversation with the announcer.

"Tyson catches fire!" said the announcer. "He'll really have to show character."

"Absolutely. Character is key. Now watch, Ndaba. See there? The footwork? This is how—*oh!*—What—What is this now?"

Mandla and I were on our feet in front of the TV next to the Old Man, all three of us shouting, "No way! No way!" Holyfield broke away from Tyson, jumping up and down in a circle, clutching the side of his head. Blood oozed through his fingers.

"He bit him! He bit him!"

The crowd at the MGM Grand went berserk as the ref came between the two fighters. Holyfield turned to go to his corner, and Tyson shoved him from behind.

"Bad form!" Madiba declared. "This is far outside Queensbury regulations."

"Oh, that's some nasty stuff in there," said the announcer. "That looked to be a bite almost."

"*Almost*?" A slow motion replay clearly showed Tyson

spit a chunk of Holyfield's ear on the floor. "*YHO! YHO! YHO!*"

The fight paused for a few minutes while they tended to Holyfield's ear, dowsing it with a water bottle.

"Granddad, do you think they'll go on?" I asked.

"Man, it's hard to say." Madiba shook his head. "There's a lot of money invested in this fight. A tremendous pressure to succeed."

The announcer made a wry comment about Holyfield's wife being a pain management specialist. The bell clanged. To everyone's surprise, the fight was going on.

"This is a real grudge match now," said the announcer, and another minute or so in, Tyson proved this correct. He bared his teeth and went for Holyfield's other ear. We were all on our feet again, hollering in five different languages.

"*Hayi-bo! Yho!*"

"Outrageous!" Madiba said. "This is not a cockfight. Show some decency! Be a man and abide by the rules."

It was all over now. Totally out of control. Dozens of people surged onto the ring, punching, bellowing, or struggling for the best camera angle. Mandla and I found all this enormously entertaining, but Madiba sat quietly in his wingback chair, observing the chaos.

"They must disqualify him," he said with genuine

sadness. "I don't know if anyone has ever been disqualified from a heavyweight title fight, but they must disqualify him. No matter how much money they've spent, this cannot be allowed to continue."

The announcer pointed out that with the cut over his right eye, Tyson couldn't have gone on much longer anyway. "That may have been the panic setting in," he said.

"What do you think?" I asked Madiba. "Did he panic, Granddad? Or was that his strategy? Like, he would lose, but people would still think he's tougher."

The Old Man shook his head. "We can't know what's in another man's mind, Ndaba. I do know that unrestrained violence is neither toughness nor strategy."

The event went down in boxing history as "The Bite Fight." In the subsequent posturing, Tyson claimed that he'd bitten Holyfield's ear in retaliation for the previous head-butting he didn't believe was accidental. He got a lot of attention, but Holyfield was the champ. Not long after the Sound and the Fury fight, Holyfield came to our house in Houghton to see Madiba again.

"Champ! How are you?" Madiba went out to greet him on the front stoop. "So good to see you!"

I always tried to hang back when a lot of cameras were around, but I craned my neck for a closer look at that half-healed ear—and yes, there was a healthy chunk of cartilage missing.

A FTER MY DAD FINISHED school, he began prac-
ticing law. Something to do with the insurance
business, I think. The Old Man got him a house in an
upscale Jewish neighborhood in Norwood, less than five
minutes from Houghton. Very decent. Very nice. It was a
three-bedroom house with a swimming pool. My brothers and I stayed with Madiba and Graça. I don't recall
any conversation suggesting otherwise. At that point,
I'd spent more years with Madiba than I'd spent with
either of my parents. I'd seen my mom only a couple
of times since I was ten. I saw my dad at family events
where I saw all my extended family. Christmas and Eas-
ter. Birthdays. That kind of thing. Functionally, on a
day-to-day basis, Madiba was my father—my provider,
my guardian, my everything—the one who stepped up
to do everything you hope a father would do.

Sometimes I found my granddad's high standards
and stiff rules hard to live with—probably because I
was such an unruly little shit in my early teens. Madiba
brought the structure and boundaries that were missing
from my early childhood. Every once in a while, when
he was tasking me about studying harder or grilling me
for mouthing off, I would start to say something stupid
and immediately realize that I wouldn't change my circumstances for anything. I was ridiculously fortunate,

and I knew it. It wasn't easy for either of us, but for the first time in my life, I felt solid ground under my feet. When I look back on those years, I'm overwhelmed with gratitude.

After Graça and Madiba were married, we moved one street over to a bigger house with more room for the expanding family, and sometimes when school was on holiday, we'd all decamp to the presidential residence in Pretoria. During apartheid, the place was called Libertas, after the Roman goddess of liberty. So that was a little ironic. When Madiba took office, he renamed the place Mahlamba Ndlopfu, which literally translated from Xitsonga is "the washing of the elephants," but it actually means "the new dawn"—the time when elephants come to the water.

Whether we were in Pretoria or at home in Houghton, Graça insisted that we all have lunch and dinner together at the table. If Madiba was traveling away from home, we might hang out in the kitchen or eat in front of the TV, but when he was there, we were all at that table, on time, all together. These family suppers were nothing like the silent meals Madiba and I shared at the long dining room table when I was in primary school. Conversation was irreverent and full of laughter. We kidded each other and even teased the Old Man when he was in the mood for it. We celebrated holidays and birthdays with big loud parties, and on the regular days, the house was bustling with comings and goings and activity.

One change that Graça made immediately was to get rid of the dinner table bell. Ringing that bell was not her style, and I was glad. When I first arrived, I thought it was great, and I was excited to ring that old bell myself, but as I got older, I started getting a vaguely *colonial master* kind of vibe off that bell, and it made me uncomfortable. I see now that it was one of the artifacts of Madiba's imprisonment; he didn't know certain things about modern manners because he'd missed this large chunk of life. He used to say, "It will probably shock many people to discover how colossally ignorant I am about simple things the ordinary person takes for granted." He'd grown up in a rural area, and then he was in the crucible of apartheid, and then he was in jail. He was very cultured, very careful about etiquette, but because he'd lost his freedom at a time before etiquette became more relaxed, he still carried himself with an old school sort of courtliness.

One day when we were eating lunch, Mama Xoli brought the phone to the dining room and handed it to him. "Her Majesty Queen Elizabeth would like to speak with you."

"Put her through," my granddad said. He took up the phone and said, "Hello? Hello, Elizabeth! How are you? Good, good. Oh, yes, I'm fine, thank you."

Graça and I looked at each other, startled to hear him address her so informally. The call went on, a casual chat from the sound of it. After he hung up and Mama Xoli took the phone away, Graça said, "Madiba, you can't just call her Elizabeth. You have to say Your Highness. There's protocol."

"What are you talking about? She calls me Nelson. We always call each other by our first names. Don't forget, I'm royalty." He smiled at me sideways like *Recognize*. "I'm a Thembu prince."

Graça laughed and said to the contrary, "You are so ungovernable."

Madiba liked to tell the story about how he first met his friend Elizabeth at Buckingham Palace years ago. "We had lunch, and after lunch we walked and walked, and then we had tea. We spent the day getting to know one another."

He finally told her, "Well, I'm going back to my hotel to rest."

She asked him, "Where are you staying."

He said, "I'm staying at the Dorchester."

"There's no Dorchester tonight," she decreed. "Tonight, you're staying here."

And he was like, "Oh. Okay."

That's how the story went, anyway, and it was a story he clearly relished telling.

"But you're not actually a prince, are you?" I said.

"Oh, yes. We are from the Royal House of the Thembus," he told me very seriously. "The first wife of the king is the great house. The second wife is the right hand house. The third wife, the left hand house, and so forth. Each house is with a different wife. The first son from the first house is the heir, but each house has its mission. The role of the second house is to step up and do anything the first house can't handle—whatever is delegated when the first house gets too busy. The third house has to get in between them sometimes because wherever men get a little taste of power, battles will be waged, and so it's gone on through the ages. We are descended from the fourth house. Our role is to be mediators who counsel the king, so when I was a young man, I was assigned to be trained as a royal advisor."

"Like with wars and stuff?"

"There's more to governing than waging wars. There's economics, infrastructure, the common good. For the old kings, it meant making sure that disputes were being settled properly. But I ran away to Johannesburg. A marriage was being arranged for me, and—oh, boy, I did not want to marry that girl. You see, my cousin Justice and I were dating these two girls, but the king didn't know this, and so when he arranged the marriage, he swapped them. Inadvertently, he arranged for us to marry each other's girlfriends. You see the difficulty."

"So you disobeyed your old man," I observed. "He didn't always know what was best for you."

Madiba knew exactly where I was going with that.

"I was a man," he said. "When you go to the mountain and become a man, then you can tell me who knows what's best for you. Until that time, you listen to your elders."

In June 1999, when I was sixteen years old, Madiba left office, wholeheartedly supporting Thabo Mbeki to succeed him. He had said from the beginning that he would serve no more than one five-year term, and he held true to that resolve. In his final speech to parliament, he talked about the new era South Africa had entered. He was intensely proud of what had been accomplished, but he gave credit for the transformation to the people of South Africa who had chosen "a profoundly legal path to their revolution." He said, "I am the product of Africa and her long-cherished dream of a rebirth that can now be realized so that all of her children may play in the sun." The Old Man was feeling buoyant, very excited about the next phase of his life, and cracked everyone up by saying, "We were able to once again increase old age pensions. I'm very excited about this. In Davos, in Switzerland, I told the plenary session that in a few months, I will be standing next to the road saying, 'Please help! Unemployed! No money and new wife!'"

He remained involved in politics, finding a new place for himself on the world stage, but he wanted to make his children and grandchildren a priority. He was still bombarded with a daily onslaught of phone calls and visitors and issues, but now he could choose which of those issues he was interested in, a luxury he never had as a sitting president—especially the first black president. For me, the upside was that we saw more of him at home. The downside was that this made it harder to get away with anything. I was beginning to chafe under Madiba's high expectations, the ten o'clock curfew, and stern lectures, and I knew that he believed world travel is an important part of a well-rounded education, so the year after he left office, Kweku and I pitched him on the idea that we and our cousin Zondwa should make our first trip to America.

I'd gone to Hong Kong with Mandla when I was thirteen. I'd also spent six weeks in Paris with Selema, my friend from way back in the days of the Gents. His mother was there as the South African ambassador, and she made sure that the trip was a good balance of reasonable running around and educational experience. I figured I was a man of the world, well able to handle myself abroad. Madiba wasn't totally convinced on that count, so when we approached him with the idea, he said, "Okay, but Mandla will go with you to look after you."

Kweku and I exchanged glances. This was not what we'd had in mind, but—whatever—we were going to ride the roller coasters in Disneyworld, and that's all we cared about.

"That's cool," we agreed. "We're down with that."

"And you should take Mbuso and Andile," said the Old Man. "Then you have someone to look after as well."

We were okay with that. Mbuso was nine, a low-maintenance little brother who would do as he was told, and seven-year-old Andile would do whatever Mbuso did. Kweku, Zondwa, and I were like the Three Musketeers, and we figured Mandla would be preoccupied with his own agenda, so we'd pretty much be free to do whatever we wanted to do as long as we kept half an eye on the little brothers. So we all went to America.

To some extent, we were right about Mandla. He had his own agenda, and it didn't include having three underage knuckleheads constantly in tow. He showed up for our big "brothers trip" with his girlfriend, which was a last minute surprise and should have been our first clue that the trip wasn't about us at all. We let that slide until we realized that he had all the money. And in America, you need a lot of money. He didn't want to give us a dime. If we wanted so much as a dollar for an ice cream, we had to plead with him, like we were petitioning the king. We were supposed to buy clothes for ourselves, but when it came time to do that, Mandla told Kweku, "You already spent your money on CDs." We started seeing how much Mandla was spending on his girlfriend and felt that we'd been completely hood-winked. So the trip ended up going kind of sideways. This was the beginning of the end of my relationship with my brother Mandla—not because of the trip budget, but because I realized he wasn't the Fresh Prince I'd idolized for so many years.

But all that aside, as long as the Three Musketeers were together, it was all good, and we did go to Disneyworld. That was the highlight. Mbuso and Andile were just the right age for Disneyworld, and the great thing about taking little kids to Disneyworld is that you have an excuse to act like a little kid yourself. We went on every ride, ate junk food, and took pictures with princesses. The whole Disney thing. It was awesome.

So toward the end of the day, we're all standing in line, waiting to get on Space Mountain. To get on Space Mountain, you know, you have to first wind back and forth in this seemingly endless queue, which the Disney design team has tried to make less seemingly endless with interesting videos and displays about space and the science of space exploration. Kweku and Zondwa and I are taking all this in, really enjoying ourselves, when the guy in front of us turns and says, "Hey, where are you guys from?"

I guess he heard us talking back and forth and not sounding exactly like the average American.

"We're from South Africa," I said, thinking he was being friendly.

"Wow," he said. "So how big do lions get?"

"What?" Kweku and I didn't get it at first.

"The lions in Africa. Like, how big are they really?"

"Bro, I don't work at the zoo," I said. "How am I supposed to know how big lions are?"

He turned away without answering that question, but I already knew the answer. We were black. We were from Africa. We must have been raised in the bush. I mean, what does Africa look like to you, if you're looking through the kaleidoscope lens of Disney circa 2001? It looks like *The Jungle Book* and *The Lion King*. It's Baloo and Mowgli. It's the jazz musician apes who say "I wanna be like you" and the Lion King holding up baby Simba as all the other animals genuflect and sing about the "circle of life." I genuinely believe this guy was trying to be friendly, chatting with us, expressing an interest in reaching across a cultural boarder, and if you had asked him, "Are you a racist?" the answer would have been a stunned and wounded, "No! Of course not! Look at me chatting with black dudes in line at Disneyworld! Doesn't that show I'm not a racist?"

I won't even pretend that I was wrapping my head around the idea of passive microaggression or systemic endemic racism at that age, but standing there in that line and later, as I flew through the solar system on Space Mountain, something started to sit weird in my gut. Something about the way Africa was perceived throughout the world. I'd seen it in Hong Kong and Paris, but couldn't put my finger on it. Now I was seeing it in America: a dynamic my teenage brain boiled down to a simple equation. On the flight home, I said to Kweku, "In the eyes of the rest of the world, it's like: Africa equals lions."

"And Johannesburg equals violence," said Kweku.

"No shit. When I tell people where I'm from, they say, 'Oh, my god, isn't it so dangerous there! So much crime. That must be so terrible.' It's always something about safari or crime. That's their whole idea of Africa."

We agreed that trying to explain that to somebody standing in line for Space Mountain was a lost cause. All the Buffalo bravado in the world doesn't make you immune to a bee sting. Taking a bite out of your opponent doesn't make you the champ. Telling someone they're wrong has never once in the history of the world convinced anyone that you're right.

"*Ulwazi alukhulelwa*," the old folks say. "One does not become great by claiming greatness."

Kweku and I knew it was going to take a lot more than that, but it took us a few more years to figure out what to do about it.

7

Isikhuni sibuya nomkhwezeli.

"A brand burns him who stirs it up."

Don't get me wrong; I loved *The Lion King*, and for real, Mbuso and Andile could watch that DVD a hundred times in a row and sing every song word for word. Same with *The Jungle Book*, to a lesser extent. No disrespect, Disney. I especially like that part in *The Lion King* where Simba, the adolescent lion (voiced by Matthew Broderick, because all the black actors were apparently unavailable that day) seeks the advice of Rafiki, a wise old mandrill (voiced by Robert Guillaume).

"I know what I have to do," says Simba, "but going back means I'll have to face my past, and I've been running from it for so long."

Swack! Rafiki bashes him over the head with a big stick.

"Ow!" says Simba. "Geeze! What was that for?"

"It doesn't matter," says Rafiki. "It's in the past."

Simba says, "Yeah, but it still hurts."

"Oh, yes," says Rafiki, "the past can hurt. But the way I see it, you can either run from it or learn from it."

On one level, it's a Disneyfied restatement of the words of the Spanish-American philosopher George Santayana: "Those who cannot remember the past are condemned to repeat it." You could definitely apply this to colonialism in general and apartheid in particular. On a more personal level, I suppose it's about the baggage we either drag through our lives or take a moment to unpack.

We didn't spend a lot of time talking through all the feelings when I was growing up. You did what you were supposed to do, because there was always a lot of stuff going on that was way bigger than your stuff, whatever your stuff happened to be. Those years are such a minefield. I dread the day Lewanika and Neema are in that phase where they're borrowing my car and telling me off and seriously imagining that they know everything, but I know that if they don't go through that, there's something wrong with them. All I can do is take that ride with them and try to remember that a lot of people cut me a lot of slack back when I was in that phase.

My dad lived nearby, but at first, I didn't see him very often. My mom was still somewhat adrift, still struggling with substance abuse and personal issues. As I got older, I started processing all the things that I'd seen and heard when I was little—stuff I'd never really processed because I was too young to understand what was happening—and it was like rebreaking a bone that hasn't mended properly. This is the problem with a culture in which children aren't allowed to ask questions. Eventually they grow up and discover they don't have any answers.

Madiba was aware of (if not exactly sensitive to) the challenges and changes I was going through as a teenager, and he made an effort to help me through it. As I got older, he invited me to travel with him more often, and there was a bit of a learning curve there. I was camera shy, but other than that, I was gung ho about being wherever we were, which was usually someplace awesome. I remember attending a soccer match with him in the late 1990s—I think it was South Africa versus the Netherlands—and as Mike drove our car out onto the field, I was getting more and more excited about meeting all these famous soccer players. As the car slowed to a stop, I jumped the gun and opened my door. I got out, and the sound of this massive crowd hit me like a tidal wave—this huge energy wave—and then the energy shifted as people realized I wasn't Madiba. It was like, *Aw, man, who's this guy? We want Mandela!* Mike was out of the car too now, standing ready to open Madiba's door for him and looking at me like, *Dude. Really?*

"Sorry, man," I said. "You forgot to tell me I should wait."

Mike opened the door for the Old Man, and then the crowd went wild for real. I physically felt this outpouring of love coming in his direction. He smiled at me and shrugged, just to let me know we were cool, and then we went over to this line of great players. I stood in awe of every one of these guys, but my granddad introduced me with great pride.

"Hello! How are you today? This is my grandson, Ndaba. He'll be a matric next year."

Matric means it's your last year of high school. In the United States, you'd be called a senior. I wore a uniform to school, of course, but I was styling on my off hours. Madiba's style was relaxed but distinguished. While he was traveling, he found a shirt he liked and bought about twenty of them in different colors. He never wore T-shirts, and my brothers and I didn't either, unless we were just chilling at home. After the Old Man wore the Springbok jersey at the match in 1995, people started giving him all kinds of jerseys. Every team wherever he went. Yankees. Chicago Bears. Both the Americans and the Portuguese gave him jerseys during the World Cup. These were super special jerseys that always had "MANDELA" written on the back. In my late teens, I sprouted up tall enough to wear them, and they became a key part of my personal style: a little bit Def Jam, a little bit humanitarian icon.

I was honing my skills with the ladies, and while Madiba was probably not the first person I'd go to for advice on that, he did offer a few guidelines. First, I was not allowed to bring a girl home after dark.

"After *Ukwaluka*," he said. "Go to the mountain. Then you're ready to be a man. Then it will be appropriate for you to have a girl join us for dinner and so forth."

Second, he expected me to be super selective about the girls I fancied.

"You must date a girl in your class," he said.

At first, I took this quite literally. I thought he was

saying that I should date a girl in my own grade at my school, but as I thought about it, I decided he must mean a girl with a similar background. So I tried to think of any girl in the world who had a background similar to mine and wasn't my cousin. This narrowed the field significantly. Over time, as I dated different girls and started experiencing the world a bit more, I gradually figured out that he wanted me to date girls for whom I had genuine respect.

"Look," said the Old Man. "You are who you are. Some women in South Africa will think that makes you the jackpot. You need someone who understands your experiences in life, someone who shares your values, someone whose ambition is equal to your own. A peer. A partner."

I had an uneasy feeling that I was hearing the same lecture my dad heard about a thousand times. I shoveled some food into my mouth and mumbled, "I thought you didn't believe in arranged marriages."

"No, I said that I did not want to marry that particular girl." His tone became crisp at the edges, the way it did when he didn't like a certain line of questioning during an interview. "Arranged marriages are there for a reason, and statistically, they are more successful, because you're not just marrying an individual. You're marrying into a family. That's how marriage is viewed in our tradition. First it's father talking to father, and then you meet the wife, and they say—*boom*—you're getting married. I ran away because they exchanged one girl for another."

"Maybe she didn't want to marry you either."

"You could be correct in that," he shrugged. "Ndaba, no one is trying to tell you who to marry. No one is telling you what to do."

That was a laugh. "Granddad, you're *always* telling me what to do."

"No, I only insist that you do your best. And if I see you doing something stupid, I tell you, 'Don't do that!' "

This sort of exchange became more and more typical. We'd sit down to watch a soccer game or boxing match, and for some reason, all his sage takes on everything started to bug me. When I was fifteen, for example, I got a puppy from the driver who took me to school and performed other daily house chores. It was a poodle. Cutest little thing. I had the puppy only for a day or two, but I was attached to it. I had committed, and not just because nothing softens the heart of a girl like a super cute puppy. The Old Man passed by my room, saw me with the puppy, and immediately shut that down.

"Oh, Ndaba. A dog? Who told you that you could keep a dog? No, no, no. That thing has to go. Get rid of it immediately."

I pleaded with him, "Granddad, please. I never asked you to let me keep any dog. This dog I really, really want to keep. I'll take good care of him. There won't be any mess or noise or anything."

"Ndaba," he said, "you see this dog? When it gets sick, you have to take it to the vet. When it's hungry, you have to buy food for it. Many people do not have these luxuries, Ndaba. Now you want to give it to a dog? Look how many people treat their dog better than they treat another human being. We won't be keeping a dog here."

I had no ready argument for all that. He made me give the dog back to the driver, who found another home for it, but I was crushed. I knew my granddad wasn't morally opposed to a person having a dog. He knew plenty of people with dogs—*his buddy Queen Elizabeth? Hello!*—and never had he judged any of them this way. The rest of the world could have as many dogs as they wanted, but not me. No dog for Ndaba. I was angry. I can't even remember the dog's name now. I just had to force myself to separate from it. It made me nuts.

By the time I was in my last year of high school, I felt compelled to argue with the Old Man, and he didn't enjoy being argued with. I guess he felt he'd done enough arguing in his life, and he was over it. Sometimes I could feel us circling each other like Holyfield and Tyson, probing for strengths and weaknesses, testing for character. Sometimes we'd get into it, and I'd go to bed regretting it hard, but when we got up in the morning it was always *mahlamba ndlopfu*—the washing of the elephants—a new dawn. But that didn't stop me from stirring something up the next day.

When we moved over to the second house in Houghton, Graça agreed that the older boys needed their space, so while some construction was being done to accommodate that, Mandla and I stayed in the first house. This was the perfect setup for sneaking a girl in, as if it was my crib and so forth, and my granddad was none the wiser. As far as I knew. Of course, in the moment, you always wish and hope and pray you'll get away with it. Once when Mandla was home from uni for the weekend, however, he caught me getting busy with a beautiful American girl. One would think he would have been on my side, but at the end of the day, Mandla was always on his own side. He didn't want me messing up his good situation or getting him in trouble with the Old Man. He seriously went off on me. Like any red-blooded male, I was trying to salvage the situation.

"Bro, c'mon. Are you kidding me right now? Bro, don't ruin this for me."

"Get her out of here!" He kept after me every five minutes until I had to give in and send the girl home.

Not long after that, I borrowed Mandla's car without asking. He was away for the weekend, and I couldn't help myself. This car was a silver Toyota Tazz the Old Man had gotten him on a trip overseas. It was all custom designed with sixteen-inch alloy wheels, BBS mags, dark tinted windows, and four twelve-inch Rockford Fosgate speakers. Top of the range. He literally converted the entire boot of the car into a giant speaker. So I felt quite chuffed cruising around in the Tazz. Unfortunately, one of Mandla's friends spotted me and called him. *Busted!*

When Mandla got back, I was watching TV with one of my boys. Mandla was seriously upset, and things got physical. He hit me in front of his girlfriend. Obviously, I couldn't tell the Old Man the whole backstory on that, so I had to make up some cock and bull fable, and I was never any good at lying to him, so I sat there feeling like he was staring laser beams through my skull.

I was so over it. All of it. Not just this incident or the dog—it was everything. I started thinking about my dad's setup just five minutes away, where I could come and go as I pleased, and no one would know or care. There was a cottage out back where I'd be able to entertain a girl if my dad was off with his mates. I didn't so much ask my dad as tell him, "Hey, I'm going to move over to your house." But you didn't tell the Old Man stuff like this. You asked. I went into his office one evening and said, "Granddad, would it be okay if I go stay with my dad for a while?"

He looked up from the book he was reading. He didn't look surprised. He didn't ask me why I wanted to leave. He didn't argue that I should stay.

"I've always been disappointed that I was not closer to your father," he said.

"But for him and me," I ventured, "maybe it's not too late."

He nodded. "Whatever you choose to do, Ndaba, you know this is your home."

"I know, Granddad. It's just for a while."

I walked out of there thinking I was finally free, and it felt great. Nobody would be breathing down my neck, telling me that what I was doing wasn't good enough, telling me to clean my room or pick up my crap. A lady came in to clean up after us. Life at my dad's house was a pretty sweet situation, hanging out, doing whatever I wanted to do and not doing anything I didn't want to do. Poor Kweku, I thought. Auntie Maki had him working away, studying and doing chores, while Dad and I lounged by the pool. My dad would get home from work, put some jazz on the stereo, take off his pants and shirt and put on shorts or his PJs. He had a lady friend—I guess we'd say "friend with benefits" these days—who came by now and then, but she seemed harmless, and I didn't much care about what they were doing anyway.

Three days a week, a lady came in to cook for us. The rest of the time, we ordered takeout. I had never once gotten takeout at my granddad's place. The Old Man had no time for that. He wanted that good old home cooking all day every day. Mama Xoli and Mama Gloria were on top of things no matter how late he worked or how many family members showed up for breakfast, lunch or dinner. At my dad's place, it was usually just him and me, sometimes my brothers, sometimes a few friends, kicking it by the pool. Nobody preached at me about politics or history. We didn't talk about much at all.

"Man, I'm spoiled by South African beer," said Dad. "Light, clean, never bitter. Just like a good woman." He laughed, and I thought, *Oh, yeah. This is gonna work out fine.*

I didn't drink with my dad, but he knew I was drinking. One night Kweku and I went out and got hammered and stumbled in about 4:30 in the morning. Dad was up watching a Mike Tyson fight. We made a perfunctory effort to hide our booze, but not very well. My pops let it slide. I vaguely remember him having a conversation about the fight with Kweku. I could hardly stand up. That little voice in my head told me, "Time for bed, buddy." I staggered to my room and passed out.

My dad was sympathetic when it came to my growing issues with Mandla. He won't listen to anyone," he said. Mandla was eager to get married, but both Dad and the Old Man gave him the same advice: "Don't rush. Finish your degree first." Mandla didn't want to hear it. He went ahead with the wedding, even though I was the only family member who attended. People kept questioning me about it, and I repeated some weak story about how they were traveling or something. When I tried to talk to Dad about it, he said, "Just focus on your studies." At first it felt good to know he was on my side, but it became uncomfortable. I would have been happier if it could have been the three of us hanging out by the pool.

Dad encouraged me to do well in school, but he didn't dog me about it constantly. If I went out at night and got a little too much party on, he didn't expect me to rock out of bed first thing in the morning to exercise and make my bed and get to school on time. The mess in my room was my own business, and the mess in his room was his business. He seemed more like the old warm, easygoing dad I remembered from

when I was little and we lived with Grandma Evelyn
in the Eastern Cape and I could stop by the grocery
store for chocolate or chips or whatever I wanted. My
friends and I spent a good many evenings floating in
the pool and getting drunk off our asses. We partied
every weekend. I pretty much blew off studying, cutting more classes than I attended, and it showed in the
miserable marks I received. When the next round of
reports came out, I was glad the Old Man was out of
the loop. I thought I could count on my dad to take it
in stride, but he didn't.

"Ndaba, you've got to do better," he warned. "I put
up with years of nagging about my own studies. I don't
need the Old Man on my back about yours."

I knew he was serious, but I also knew he wasn't
actually going to do anything to slow my roll, so we
were still cool. Auntie Maki was pleased that Dad
and I were finally making an attempt at building a
relationship. She encouraged him to tell me more
about his own childhood, which was pretty screwed
up. Madiba and Grandma Evelyn were divorced
when my dad was eight years old, largely because
Grandma Evelyn was completely into the Jehovah's
Witness faith and not down with all the ANC stuff.
She believed Madiba should allow God to correct
the wrongs in the world, and she didn't want to live

with the constant threats. She hated having to constantly run away and hide from authorities. From the very start of primary school, Dad and his big brother Thembi and little sister Maki had to adopt fake names in order to go to school, knowing they must never tell anyone who they really were.

Even after Madiba married Mama Winnie, the police harassed and threatened Evelyn because she was his first wife and had his three oldest children. Madiba was Public Enemy Number 1, and they were desperate to draw him out. Eventually, Grandma Evelyn fled with her children to Swaziland, where they lived as refugees until Madiba was found and arrested. Dad was twelve when Madiba went to jail. He was nineteen when Thembi was killed.

"After Thembi died," Dad told me, "I get a letter from your granddad. He says, 'I hate to give lectures, Kgatho, but your big bro is gone, now you better step up your game!'"

I might have laughed at the notion of the Old Man holding back from a good lecture, but as I grew to know my father, I was coming to an uncomfortable conclusion: My granddad had failed my dad in many of the same ways my dad had failed me. I've seen that letter fairly recently. It's archived in Madiba's book *Conversations with Myself*. I find it quite stunning for several reasons: the tone, the content, and the timing—just fifteen days after Uncle Thembi's death—but also the foresight. At that moment in time, there was little hope that Madiba himself had any future at all beyond Robben Island, but he expressed a prescient and optimistic view of the future and was determined to see my father find a place in it.

July 28, 1969

I hate giving lectures, Kgatho, even to my own children and I prefer discussing matters with everyone on a basis of perfect equality, where my views are offered as advice which the person affected is free to accept or reject as it pleases him. But I will be failing in my duty if I did not point out that the death of Thembi brings a heavy responsibility on your shoulders. Now you are the eldest child, and it will be your duty to keep the family together and to set a good example for your sisters, to be a pride to your parents and to all your relatives. This means that you will have to work harder on your studies, never allow yourself to be discouraged by difficulties or setbacks, and never give up the battle even in the darkest hour.

So no pressure, right?

Remember that we live in a new age of scientific achievement, the most staggering of which is the recent landing of man on the moon. That is a sensational event that will enrich man's knowledge of the universe and that may even result in a change or modification of many fundamental assumptions in many fields of knowledge. The younger generation must train and prepare themselves so that they can easily grasp the far-reaching repercussions of developments in the realm of space. This is an era of intense and vicious competition in which the richest rewards are reserved for those who have undergone the most thorough training and who have attained the highest academic qualifications in their respective fields. The issues that agitate humanity today call for trained minds and the man who is deficient in this respect is crippled because he is not in possession of the tools and equipment necessary to ensure success and victory in the service of country and people. To lead an orderly and disciplined life, and to give up the glittering pleasures that attract the average boy, to work hard and systematically in your studies throughout the year, will in the end bring you coveted prizes and much personal happiness. It will inspire your sisters to follow the example of their beloved brother, and they will benefit greatly through your scientific knowledge, vast experience, diligence and achievements. Besides, human beings like to be associated with a hardworking, disciplined and successful person and by carefully cultivating these qualities you will win yourself many friends.

The strangest thing about this letter is that I see both the man who failed in raising my father and the man who succeeded in raising me. I know Thembi's death gutted my granddad. I know he was in unimaginable pain. He had to have known that my dad was suffering the same debilitating grief. Couldn't he have found one word of comfort to offer? Or would that have cracked some floodgate that kept his own grief from killing him? Was he forced to keep this stone-cold fix on the future so he could physically keep fighting? If that's the case, though they could not have known this at the time, it was not my father Madiba was fighting for. It was me.

Apartheid did not willingly let go of its last generations. They emerged from it free but deeply damaged. You can't break a man's hands and then tell him, "Hey, you still have toes, right? So if you would only work hard enough, you could still be a concert pianist." The opportunities available to me in the first thirty years of my life and the opportunities available to my father in the first thirty years of his life are not even close to being in the same stratosphere. I learned many important life lessons from my granddad, but here's something I learned from my dad: No one who was born with less opportunity than you is asking for your pity. They don't need your charity. They are asking for your respect, an honest recognition of the mountain they have already climbed just to survive as far as the point at which others started.

We all need and deserve the same thing: a fair lane of opportunity in which to reach our full potential. Even if it is true that all men are created equal, the world quickly tips the balance to alter that equality. Two evenly matched boxers are not in a fair fight if one of them has a cinder block chained to his ankle. If his only opportunity to survive is to pick up the cinder block and use it as a weapon, why should anyone be surprised if he does that? The Truth and Reconciliation Commission was an enormous step forward for the people of South Africa. We took ownership of the moral aspect of apartheid, but we've yet to address the economic aspect, in my opinion.

The Bantu Education Act of 1953 was pitched to parliament by Dr. Hendrik F. Verwoerd, Minister of Native Affairs, as a measure that was both Christian and compassionate: "There is no space for [a non-white person] in the European Community above certain forms of labor.... Until now he has been subjected to a school system which drew him away from his community and misled him by showing him the greener pastures of European society where he is not allowed to graze."

The whole Bantu thing promoted an image of black Africans as heathen savages who should be firmly but lovingly domesticated and Christianized by their white benefactors, and a lot of people still see things this way. As recently as January 2018, Donald Trump, the sitting president of the United States, made reference to "shithole countries" in Africa, saying Nigerian people would never "go back to their huts" if they had the opportunity to live in the United States. It's virtually impossible to watch late night television for fifteen minutes without seeing a plea from an NGO depicting African children with wide eyes and swollen bellies, marketing the idea that the proper response to this is a donation to their cause rather than a redress of political and socioeconomic wrongs that continue robbing the richest continent on this planet of her diamonds, gold, and oil.

My father was given an extraordinary opportunity to change his circumstances in the latter part of his life, but hundreds of thousands of people educated in the Bantu system, which unabashedly trained black people to be a servant class to white people, are still in the work force doing exactly what the Bantu system hardwired them to do, seeing themselves exactly as the Bantu system hardwired them to see themselves. And if you think the legislative dismantling of the Bantu system—or of segregation in general—magically negates its far-reaching culturally toxic effects, then I must ask you: How big do the lions get in your neighborhood?

We run from the past. Or we learn from it. During that short time I lived with my father, I was still running from my past. I just didn't run quite fast enough.

To absorb the full impact of The Story of Ndaba's Epic Crash and Burn, you must understand that my granddad read the African newspapers every morning without fail. All eight regional papers. Front to back. Every day. After breakfast, he sat in the lounge in his favorite wingback chair. I was always welcome to join him, but I couldn't just take the sports section or the comics page; I had to take the whole paper, and when he was ready for that paper, I had to hand it over. Occasionally, he pointed out an article about an event that he thought I should be aware of or responded out loud to an editorial, either agreeing with great enthusiasm or disagreeing with great vehemence. He also watched the local news every evening, and that habit is still ingrained in me. To this day, regardless of the constant stream of news on my smart phone, I don't feel quite right if I haven't seen the evening news on TV.

But the papers. Those are key to this story.

One afternoon, I was out enjoying the pleasant weather and sharing a nice fat spliff with a few friendly chaps about three blocks from our high school. Some dudes cruised by, and I recognized one of them as an eleventh grader with whom Zondwa had kind of an ongoing tussle. We thought about diving for cover, but we'd seen this same fellow at a recent mash up—at his sister's house, no less. I'm talking bongs, beer funnels while they hold you upside down, that sort of thing. Someone said, "He wouldn't rat us out after that piss up, would he?" And we all agreed, "No, no. Of course, he wouldn't." But of course, he did. I suppose they figured that kicking our asses would be a lot of work and probably not end well for them, but they could seriously mess us up if they went into school and reported to the authorities that I was a few blocks up the street smoking reefer. The next day, I was called out of history class and questioned us about the incident. I remained silent, but a couple of these other chaps cracked like chicken eggs, and then it was over for everybody. We got "suspension expulsion," which means you're sent home for a week, and when you come back, the slightest infraction, even the tiniest step outside the rules means immediate expulsion.

I was staying with my dad at the time, and my dad was a hustler who grew up in the street and knew the drill. He didn't get mad at me. He was irritated about the logistical hassle, but not really angry. Probably not all that surprised.

"Ndaba, seriously?" He rolled his eyes. "Okay. We've got this. It's a situation, but we've got it. I'll go to the school and deal with it. It's fine. Main thing is, I am not gonna let your granddad find out about it."

That weekend, it was reported in the Johannesburg paper that a grandchild of former president Nelson Mandela was involved in a drug-related incident and expelled from school. They didn't say my name, and several of my cousins attended the same school, but I was the one already known for blazing mad joints, so the time bomb was ticking. My dad tried to run interference. He went to my granddad's secretary, pleading my case. "Zelda, please. He's a good kid. He just screwed up this one time. There's no need to upset the Old Man." Dad did everything he could to make sure Madiba didn't see that particular paper, but I knew he was going to see it. He saw every paper. Front to back. Every day.

I knew I would have to tell him, and on one level I was glad, because trying to keep it from him felt like hell. The only way to have it be over was to face up to it, and I desperately wanted it to be over.

"Oh, Ndaba." He sat in his chair with the paper folded between his hands. "Is this true?"

"Yes, Granddad."

It was hard to find words to explain the situation without sounding like I was trying to weasel out of it. He had no time for people trying to make excuses. He sat in his chair, listening in that deeply listening Madiba way as I floundered through the whole sordid tale.

"Granddad, I'm so sorry."

"Oh, Ndaba, I can't believe this. I'm shocked. This is so below you."

"I know, Granddad. I'm sorry."

"I can't believe you would do such a thing. Are you serious about your life? Do you understand the nature of the opportunities extended to you with your name? There are opportunities to help people—to do great things—and there are equal opportunities to burn it all to the ground. To humiliate the people who love and care for you. Your name is your name, but who are *you*? You have a choice. Every minute of every day, the choice is yours."

He was angry, but more than that, he was deeply

disappointed. After a while, he told me to go. Walking out of that room, leaving my granddad with this leaden expression of sadness on his face, I felt like I'd been punched in the throat. But I was determined to fix this. I would pass my matric, for starters. After that I'd be going to the mountain, and that would make me a man in his eyes. He'd be proud of me. I would redeem myself. Meanwhile, I'd lay low. Stay under the radar. Try not to stir things up.

The matric was not a huge success, but I scraped together a passing grade and figured, *It is what it is*. My score wasn't high enough to get into University of Cape Town, which would have been my first choice. I had no idea what I might be interested in studying at a fallback school, so I pitched my granddad on the idea of a gap year, but he shut that down hard.

"No, no, no," he said. "Straight to education. Don't play around."

"Granddad, all my friends are taking gap years—going overseas, working, backpacking."

"Well, maybe they can afford it."

"If you'd let me get a job, I could pay for it myself!"

"I mean they can afford time away from their studies. Clearly, you can not."

I trudged off to Rand Afrikaans University and half-heartedly declared a major in psychology. I decided that was not for me and switched to math and accounting. Not for me. I started politics, and that was more interesting, but not as interesting as going to clubs, sleeping in, and chatting up pretty girls who were up to the task of doing my homework. I hardly ever went to a lecture and never turned in an assignment, but I made a lot of friends and a lot of friends of friends, including Trevor Noah, who was hosting a radio show and working as an actor on a soap opera. I thought this was cool, but I wasn't that motivated. I told myself that if the Old Man wasn't going to give me a gap year, I would bloody well give myself one.

I lived in residence during the week, and weekends were party time, so I didn't go home very often, but when I did go home, I went to Houghton. My dad was always off with his mates on weekends, and he was not distressed to see me go back to living with Madiba and Graça. Mama Xoli was glad to have me back, as always. The Old Man provided me with a car—the cheapest little hatchback on the market—but he took it away from me when my half term results came back.

"No more privileges," he said. "Ndaba, this is not acceptable."

Out of six subjects, I had written only one of my exams. I had scored an F7, which meant I wouldn't be allowed to return. Turns out you had to have a minimum level of credits in order to study at the institution. I didn't even know this was the case. That's how much I cared. My main concern was getting to enjoy my holiday. I was happily hanging out with my friend Selema when I got a call from Zelda, the secretary. Madiba had instructed her to arrange a meeting with the dean. I was to attend, present myself properly, throw myself on their mercy and pledge to get my act together. The meeting went off as he intended it to. I trudged back for the second half term, and he dogged me from a distance.

"Where's your report? Did you write your calculus test? When can I see your marks? This is not acceptable, Ndaba! You're capable of much better than this." And so on and so forth while I performed an elaborate sort of shell game, trying to show him only the passing marks. When he got on my case, I said, "Why is it that I have to do as I'm told. Where would we all be right now if you had always done as you were told?"

When I said things like that, the Old Man sat there listening in that still, silent way. He didn't bother to point out to me the difference between his resistance and my rebellion. Maybe he knew that I was about to discover for myself that resistance in the right ways, at the right times, and for the right reasons makes us stronger, while flailing, selfish, anger-driven rebellion makes us weak. I hadn't yet figured out that if your freedom casts yourself and those who love you into a prison of worry and chaos, you're probably not doing freedom right.

Just before I turned eighteen, my dad went to Madiba to get the ball rolling on the whole going to the mountain of it all. I wasn't in on this discussion. I was just hanging out watching TV when Mandla came in and said, "Dad and I decided it's time for you to go to the mountain. You're going next week." Just like that. That's how they do you. They don't want you to think too much about getting your penis cut. This is an off-putting idea. It's hardcore. It was not high on the list of things I wanted to do. My birthday is in December, and most of my friends at the time were Zulu and Sotho, tribes that have moved away from this particular tradition and don't really do it anymore. So they were all going on holiday, and I was going to the mountain to get my penis cut. I was ambivalent, as any young man would be in those circumstances, but I knew there was no discussing it. If the men in my family decided it was my time to go, it was my time to go.

My dad went into Madiba's office, and he was in there a long time. Long enough for me to think about it. I knew what this would mean to my granddad, what a huge deal it was to everyone in our family. It wouldn't be so bad. I'd be able to bring girls to lunch. I could come and go as I pleased. The Old Man and my dad and Mandla would have to respect me as an equal. I could be down with that. The respect. Respect would be nice, I decided.

My dad came out of Madiba's office, and he did not look happy. He said, "Your granddad says you're not going."

"What?"

"He said no. He said, 'This boy is not ready.' So that's it."

And that was it. The Old Man was not going to change his mind. Dad and Mandla couldn't just take me anyway, because my granddad would certainly figure it out, and that would make it worse.

I was like, "Oh, well. If that's what the Old Man says, we have to respect his decision." I won't lie. My initial reaction was, *Yeeeeeesss! Thank you, God!* It was a rush of relief. But while I was on holiday—the quintessential eighteenth birthday holiday, where you get all kinds of party on and nobody threatens your genitals with a sharp instrument—I started feeling weirdly disappointed. I knew my cousins who were my age and everyone back in Qunu would expect me to be there and ask why I wasn't. I didn't know how to explain it. I thought about the initiates gathering in the dusk on the rolling plains. I could almost hear the music.

8

Intyatyambo engayi kufa ayibonakali.

"The flower that never dies is invisible."

I was not a big reader during my school days. Beyond the prescribed reading for school, I read comics. The first book I really devoured purely because I wanted to was *The Alchemist* by Paulo Coelho. Auntie Maki gave it to me when I was in high school, at a time when things were rather going off the rails and people who loved me were starting to worry.

She said, "It's about a shepherd who goes on a quest to find a great treasure that was revealed to him in a dream." But of course, if you have read this book, you know it's about much more than that. The shepherd's quest got me interested, but it was the deeper meaning of this story that resonated and refused to let me go. Back then I hardly ever finished a book, but I finished this one because I liked the way it spoke to the way we treat others and the way we interpret our own dreams and aspirations, which are shockingly easy to discard. The shepherd's journey was the journey of my own life. I could see it even then.

At the start of *The Alchemist*, young Santiago falls asleep in an abandoned church and dreams about a treasure hidden near the pyramids in Egypt, and he's determined to go find it. An elderly friend introduces him to the idea of Personal Legend—your blessing, your path, your passion—and says that all children know their Personal Legend, but as we grow up, people constantly tell us that our quest is silly or impractical or above our reach. And then, as we get older, we compound these doubts with "layers of prejudice, fear and guilt" until the Legend is crushed into the farthest, darkest corner of the soul. Unseen. Unheard. But it can still be felt. It's still there.

After my disastrous "gap year," I found myself back

at home with my granddad, sorting through my options. He suggested I return to high school, to the point when things went off the rails. This idea was not particularly attractive to me.

I said to Aunt Maki, "I'd feel like an idiot, going back to repeat my final year of matric."

"You won't repeat it," she said. "You'll do it differently this time. If you're smart."

"I could retake my matric," I said. "I know I could get a higher score. Then I could go to Cape Town, like I wanted to in the first place."

We decided together that the best course was for me to go to Damelin College and refresh that last year of high school. I was down with this, because Damelin wasn't the typical highly regimented South African high school where you wear a uniform and comply with a lot of rules stemming from whatever religion runs the school. At Damelin, you could take high school or college courses or a combination of the two. You could wear whatever you bloody pleased and smoke in the courtyard on breaks. It was the school where a lot of "troubled" kids were sent. Yes, let's use the word "troubled" because it would be wrong to say "bad kids" or "fuck ups." I don't believe that everyone who fucks up is automatically bad, and I'm certain that a lot of bad kids go through school and never make a false step.

In any case, Damelin was a good choice for me. I did do far better on the matric. I scored high enough to go on to university in Pretoria, which is known for their Politics and International Relations department. I had become increasingly fascinated by world politics, sitting with my granddad, reading the newspaper, and listening to his take on the volatile state of global relations.

At the end of 2002, the president of the United States, George W. Bush, had basically given the finger to the United Nations (UN) Security Council. He claimed that Iraq was developing WMDs (weapons of mass destruction) and used this as justification for launching a full-scale invasion of Iraq, even though the UN inspectors said there was no evidence that Iraq had WMDs. The secretary-general of the UN at that time was Kofi Atta Annan, a diplomat from Ghana. The Old Man took this very personally.

He said, "I have to wonder if Bush found it easier to disregard the United Nations because the present secretary-general is an African."

"Granddad, if they invade, will that mean the US— and the UK too, because it's Blair as well—are they no longer South Africa's allies?"

"The United States of America is a great country. We have many, many friends there and in the United Kingdom, but let's be real, the US has committed atrocities and never expressed one whit of sorrow for it. Think about the atom bombs in Hiroshima and Naga- saki. Ndaba, who do you think those bombs were really aimed at?"

"The Soviet Union."

"Yes! The intention was to say, 'Here! You see what happens to you if you get to cross purposes with us.' They are so arrogant—not the people, but the government— they would kill innocent people to demonstrate their power to the rest of the world."

In January 2003, Madiba made statements on national TV and radio and gave a blowtorch of a speech to the International Women's Forum. He was angry, and he didn't hold back. When I watched the speech on YouTube, I saw the pugilist in him come out. The rock hammerer. The freedom fighter.

"George Bush as well as Tony Blair are undermin- ing an idea that was sponsored by their predecessors," he said. "They do not care. Is it because the secretary- general of the United Nations is now a black man?"

The large audience cheered.

"They never did that when secretary-generals were white. What is the lesson of them acting outside of the United Nations? Are they saying any country which believes that they will not be able to get the support of the other countries are entitled to go outside the

United Nations and ignore it? Or are they saying, 'We, the United States of America, are the only superpower in the world now. We can act as we like'? Are they saying this is a lesson we should follow? Or are they saying, 'We are special. What we do should not be done by anybody'?"

He laid out his theory about Nagasaki and Hiroshima and pretty much flamed George W. Bush.

"Who are they now to pretend that they are the policemen the world? What I'm condemning is that one power with a president who has no foresight—who cannot think properly—is now ready to plunge the world into a holocaust. And I'm happy that the people of the world, especially those of the United States of America, are standing up and opposing their own president. I hope that opposition will one day make him understand that he has made the greatest mistake of his life in trying to bring about carnage and to police the world without any authority from the international body. It is something we have to condemn without reservation."

The speech was all over the Internet the next day. Headlines naturally latched onto the harshest remarks, but that was fine with the Old Man; he didn't regret a word of it. He told me that George H. W. Bush—the former president, father of George W.—called that evening.

"What did he say?" I asked.

"Oh, he asked me in a very civil manner, 'Please, Mr. Mandela, do not say any more bad things about my son.'"

"And what did you say?"

"I told him, 'Don't worry about it. I've said my piece. That's all I have to say about the matter.'"

Having been on the receiving end of the Old Man's anger, I almost felt sorry for both Bushes, Junior and Senior.

DURING MY FIRST YEAR at the university—the first year that mattered, anyway—I was primarily focused on my studies, but I also made an effort to get reacquainted with my mom, who had settled down somewhat. I'd seen her only a few times during high school, but that sojourn with my father had opened my eyes to some of the hard realities of my mom's life.

My dad had told me, "The Old Man set her up in the East Rand—house, job, all set up. But she's far away from me. I'm a man. What do you expect? She was angry all the time. She wanted to be with her family. So she goes back to Soweto. The Old Man is like, 'What, she doesn't appreciate what I've done for her?' And maybe she doesn't. Maybe she would have appreciated not being told where to go and what to do. See, Ndaba, this is the disconnect—the Old Man, he's a great man, but he doesn't understand things like this. He's great at running the country. Not so great at running a family."

I stopped by my mother's house one day, and she was glad to see me. She cooked for me and talked to me about her job as a social worker and asked me about my classes and the girls I dated. It was small talk. We didn't revisit the past or delve into any big issues of why things went down the way they did. We were just hanging out together, eating supper, watching TV, reestablishing a comfortably grown-up version of the bond we had when I was a little boy. She let me be me; I let her be her. We laughed a lot. I had totally forgotten how funny and lighthearted she could be when she was happy. She'd tease and prank me and tell hilarious stories about people and places in her life. It was a good place to begin a new relationship. I assumed there would be plenty of time for that.

A few weeks later, I stopped by again, and then I made it a habit to come and see her once a month or so. One day, I came to my mother's house, and Aunt Lucy was plaiting Mom's hair. It looked strange. Aunt Lucy kept combing all this white, flaky skin from my mother's head, like dandruff except—it was just strange. The next time I came to see my mom, I could see that she was losing weight. She didn't tell me she was sick, never even hinted that she was scared or depressed or hurting, but one day Aunt Lucy called me and said, "Oh, Ndaba. She's not well. She went to hospital and stayed there for a week. They gave her pills and sent her home. They said there's nothing more they can do."

"Tell her I'm coming," I said.

My mind went immediately to tuberculosis. Maybe pneumonia. I went to see her in Soweto, and she was not in a good state. She had a relentless, wracking cough. A strange white rash had broken out on her temples and forehead.

"I'm worried about her," I told Mandla. "Something is very wrong."

"She won't get the best care at the free hospital in Soweto," he said. "You must take her to a private hospital."

That sounded like a good idea. I did some research. Mandla helped me make arrangements, and we moved her to a private hospital closer to Houghton, thinking that would make all the difference. I thought she'd get better and go home again, and meanwhile, I'd be able to see her every other day. This was my plan.

Standing in the hallway outside my mother's hospital room, I asked the new doctor, "How long do you think it'll take for her to get well?"

"Get well?" The doctor looked at me with a quizzical expression. "Ndaba, did you know that your mother is HIV positive?"

"No," I said. That was suddenly the only word in my head. *No. No. No.*

"Pneumocystis pneumonia is caused by a fungus," she said. "It's very common. Virtually everyone is exposed to it by the time they're three or four. A person with a healthy immune system might never know they have it. But someone with your mother's condition, a person with HIV..."

She kept talking, but it was just a lot of noise and words and numbers and information on a chart, and I was concentrating on keeping my knees from buckling under me. At some point, I just turned and walked away. I broke down crying. I went back to my mother's room and raged at her. "How could you not tell me this? Why didn't you tell me?" She sat on the edge of her chair, staring at the floor. I could see the weight of abject shame and isolation like a physical burden on her narrow shoulders. It was one of the saddest moments of my life.

My mom went back to Soweto, but she rapidly got sicker and sicker. I brought her back to the private hospital so she would be closer to home. Every day that I could be there, I went and sat with her, and every night

I had to drink myself to sleep. I couldn't smoke enough weed to dull this pain. We sat for long hours without speaking. There was nothing to say now. There was only however many days I could stay by her side and hold her hand in mine, and so I sat there, and the weeks went by, and my mother died on July 13, 2003. It's very difficult for me to talk about it. I'd rather tell you the rest of the story about the Zulu Woman and the Accommodating River.

Remember, the woman says, "River, give me back the child I lost long ago." And the river says, "Cut out your heart and give it to me." And she does. She casts her heart into the river, so the only way she can go on living is to go live in the river with her heart, leaving the baby boy with his aunties on the shore. Every night, while the river god is sleeping, the aunties wade into the water with the baby so his mother can nurse him and play with him, and when he grows up, he devises a plan to rescue her. The Zulu woman's baby, who became a boy, who became a man, gets the people from the village to come with him to the river. He loops one end of a rope around a tree and ties the other end around his middle. He tells his friends, "Now, when I get my arms around my mother, you pull with all your strength." But the river god overhears this, and he is a jealous god. Just as the young man gets his arms around his beautiful mother, she turns into a sleek silver trout and disappears into the endless stream.

I was gutted by my mother's death. The sadness was exhausting. And I was angry. I couldn't even wrap my head around the fact that she'd chosen not to tell me something so important. Other people most certainly knew—the other doctors and nurses in Soweto, my aunts, her friends—and no one saw fit to tell me this? They all thought it was better for me to be blindsided? Or did they actually think I would never find out? HIV/AIDS was still something no one was willing to talk about. I stared at the newspaper reports about my mother's death. The family's official press release stated that she had died of pneumonia. A week later, Auntie Maki and I had a terrible falling out that started with her insisting on taking Mbuso and Andile to our granddad's birthday party. I thought this was very wrong, and I told her so.

"These two children lost their mother one week ago! You don't take them to a party."

"Everyone else is going," she said. "Who's going to look after them?"

She said it would be good for them. Robert De Niro was going to be there. Lots of press. People would wonder if they weren't there for Madiba's birthday celebration. It turned into a big tug of war, and I lost. She told Mbuso and Andile to get in the car, and they did as they were told. The whole thing made me even more heart-sick and angry—at Auntie Maki, at the world, at life.

"My mother died while I was in prison," my grand-dad told me as I helped him out to sit in the yard. "I came in from the quarry one day. Someone handed me a telegram from your dad. My mother had died of a heart attack. Her burial was my responsibility. I was her only son. Her eldest child. I was not permitted, of course. It made me question this path I'd taken—the difficulty my choices had caused her."

I didn't have an answer to that. Frankly, none of that was helpful. I wished we could just sit quietly. It didn't occur to me then that he might have been trying to tell me that he understood this feeling of powerlessness that overwhelmed me because the stigma surrounding HIV/AIDS was as unyielding as stone walls and iron bars. My mother passed away in 2003, twenty years after the human immunodeficiency virus was identified, and we—as a family, as a nation, as a global community—were still utterly unable to have an honest conversation about it. The stigma overpowered common sense, over-powered common decency, overpowered love. And I had just witnessed up close how that stigma could kill a person as effectively as the disease itself.

"When a man's mother passes away, this causes him to reevaluate his life," said the Old Man.

He was right about that, I realized. Not in that moment, maybe, but over the following year. You see, somewhere in all that mess, I relocated my Legend. The pieces were coming together—that moment in Disneyworld, that eye-opening time spent with my father, everything I'd seen and heard in my life with my granddad—it was still there. Kweku and I started talking about a concrete structure for the organization that would become Africa Rising, imagining a vehicle for the next generation to build on the cultural and sociopolitical progress Madiba and his generation had set in motion.

"We want to address the stature of Africa on the world stage," I told my granddad. "And we have to address AIDS. We have to go there."

"It's a difficult problem," he said. "We're faced with a conservative community. You remember the lady in KwaZulu-Natal just a few years ago—murdered—stoned to death by her own neighbors when she confessed to being HIV positive."

"I know. I remember. And that's not an isolated case. I understand why people are afraid to talk about it. That's the first thing that has to change."

"Ndaba, I have tried. All the way back in 1991, I went to Mpumalanga and spoke to the people. I said to the parents, 'We are facing an epidemic. You must teach your children about safe sex. You must talk about contraception.' I told them their government and their community must work together for the good of their children. I could see in their faces, they were revolted by what I was saying. They were angry. 'How can you talk like this! You're encouraging prostitution among our children!' In Bloemfontein, the principal of the school— a woman with a university degree—she said, 'Madiba, you mustn't say these things. You'll lose the election.' I knew that she was correct. And I was not keen to lose that election. I had to abandon it, Ndaba. But in 1999, in my last media address as president, I did tell them that initiatives must be advanced. Educating the public, making AZT more affordable—these are expensive programs. You can't expect it to happen all at once."

I understood what my grandfather was saying, and I knew that he had done more than anyone else ever did before him, but it wasn't enough.

"Nothing will ever change if we can't talk about it, Granddad. If a woman can't tell her neighbors without fearing for her life—if a mother can't tell her son— nothing changes. I can't accept that."

He listened and nodded.

I continued my studies, focused on getting my degree. I knew that was the first step to whatever came next. I also knew that the Old Man was committed to changing the culture of silence and stigma that provided such fertile ground for HIV/AIDS in South Africa.

The summer after my mother passed away, something huge happened. Just a few months before she died, The Clash front man Joe Strummer passed away suddenly, and one of his last projects was a collaboration with U2's Bono on the song "46664 (Long Walk to Freedom)"—a tribute to my granddad and the centerpiece of an epic "46664" concert series to raise funds and awareness for HIV/AIDS worldwide. This identifying number was assigned to the Old Man when he was taken to Robben Island, the 466th prisoner in 1964. They gave him that number, thinking they had power over him, and he reclaimed it in 2003, wanting to remind people that the real power is in their hands.

Rolling out the concert plans, he said, "I cannot rest until I am certain that the global response is sufficient to turn the tide of the epidemic."

The first "46664" concert was set to happen in Cape Town on November 29, 2003—a week before my twenty-first birthday. I was getting more and more excited as the summer went by and the lineup got more and more mind-blowing. Peter Gabriel, Robert Plant, Beyoncé, Brian May and Roger Taylor of Queen, Angelique Kidjo, Ladysmith Black Mambazo, The Who, Yvonne Chaka Chaka—even the Soweto Gospel Choir was in there for

Mama Xoli. But let's be real. Beyoncé, man. I was going to meet Beyoncé.

The day of the event, the Old Man took the stage at Green Point Stadium in front of 18,000 concertgoers and millions more watching on TV around the world. He said, "When the history of our time is written, will we be remembered as the generation who turned our backs in the moment of a global crisis, or will it be recorded that we did the right thing? We have to rise above our differences and combine our efforts to save our people."

It was a great moment. Beyoncé was there. I wasn't.

See, just a few weeks earlier, because we were approaching my twenty-first birthday, my father again raised the subject of my going to the mountain.

This time, the Old Man said, "Yes. He's ready." So I went.

9

Ukwaluka.

"Going to the Mountain"

Qunu sits about an hour from the coast in the Eastern Cape province. This was the place Madiba loved best, the home of his happiest childhood memories. We always went there in December, to the house that was a replica of the prison warden's house, so over the years, I grew to love it there too. The rolling hills were brilliant green in the spring and faded to rich amber and brown during the hottest part of the summer. On the horizon, between the village and the distant mountains, rocky outcroppings, boulders, and scarps jut into the landscape. The village itself is a picturesque collection of little brick houses and rondavels, hyperefficient circular cottages and outbuildings with thatched or tin roofs. (I'm looking forward to the rondavel fad, which is sure to replace the current "tiny home" fad soon.) At the edge of the town is the cemetery where my great-grandparents and other family members are buried.

As we made the long, scenic drive, Granddad pointed out his favorite landmarks. "See the flat rocks over there? We used to slide down those smooth rocks when I was a boy. Slide down again and again until our backsides were too sore to slide any more. And this over here—all of this was farmland then." Over here was the field where a donkey threw him in a thorn bush. Over there was the stream where he and his friends swam and caught fish. It's a rural area with farms and dairies scattered hither and yon, so every once in a while, we'd have to stop and allow for cows crossing the road, and this was the Old Man's cue to tell us about drinking warm milk straight from the udder and about the deeply significant connection between the Xhosa and the cattle that, for many generations, kept them well fed and provided a solid source of wealth. He took his role in tending the family's cattle and sheep very seriously when he was a boy, but like the shepherd Santiago in *The Alchemist*, he knew he would have to leave them someday.

In Qunu, they still love to tell a story about a white chap whose motorbike broke down as he was riding by the village on his way across the vast rolling hills. This was quite an exciting event, so the village children all ran out to spectate.

One kid steps up and says, "May I be of help?"

"You speak English!" The cyclist is surprised but glad to have a hand at fixing the motorbike, which is soon good to go. The cyclist thanks the kid and hands him three pennies.

"Thank you," says the little dude. "One for each of my sisters and one for my school fees."

"What's your name?"

"Nelson."

To keep it simple, he gave the cyclist the name he'd been given in school, but the kid's birth name was Rolihlahla, which basically means "troublemaker" and translates literally to "the one who tugs the branches of a tree." I love that name, because it so perfectly suits my granddad, but so does his manhood name, Dalibhunga ("convener of the dialogue"), which he was given at the time of his circumcision.

I looked forward to receiving my manhood name, mostly because that would mean the ordeal was almost over. I was gratified to hear Madiba say he believed I was finally ready to go to the mountain, but I have to admit, I was starting to get nervous on the way there. The *Ukwaluka* is a hardcore test of courage and the source of a lot of controversy. Every year we hear about incidents in which initiates have been disfigured or suffered the loss of their genitals or even died of complications and infections. There was a period when the government tried to regulate how the circumcisions were being done and provided stipends to people who were supposedly qualified to do the procedure, but that opened the door for a bad element—people who were in no way qualified but obtained the government certification, doing it for the money with no reverence for the tradition—and the result was a terrible spate of botched circumcisions. Hundreds of initiates died. Others were left disfigured in a way that prompted them to take their own lives.

Even when every precaution is taken, things can go badly, and the initiates are way out in the countryside, far from medical help. One of the initiates in Mbuso's group went into some kind of respiratory distress days after the circumcision. I had a car, so they asked me to rush the guy to the hospital, and I drove all the way at top speed, but it was too late. By the time I got to the clinic in Idutwya, he had passed away in the backseat of my car. I felt such sorrow for his family. The incident shook me to the core. In that moment, I realized that my grandfather didn't hold me back as a punishment; it was for my own safety. This is not something one dares to approach in a reckless or casual manner. It's imperative that the initiate be ready for what he is about to endure and that he goes into it with his *khanki*—advocates who'll stand by him the whole time. Throughout the month-long ritual, the initiates—the *Abakhwetha*—are tested to physical and psychological extremes.

At the end of November, I finished writing my exams, and then my dad and Mandla drove me to the site about 30 km from our house in Qunu, just outside of Idutwya. I was accompanied by Dad, Mandla, and my grand-dad's cousin Zuko Dani, because you need an elderly man who's familiar with the details of tradition and can talk you through each step. Madiba provided the ceremonial blanket, two bottles of brandy, and payment for the *ingcibi*, the gentleman who does the cutting. I had already seen a doctor, who inspected my organ and provided a notice that said I was in good health and okay to go to the mountain. It's not a literal mountain, by the way. That's a figure of speech. My group, which included twenty or so initiates, gathered in a secluded village on a hillside. I was glad to have two of my cousins with me. If you're born to a royal house, the tradition is to go in accompanied by cousins, young men close to your age whom you can depend on for comradeship, courage, strength and support.

So here we are. Crack of dawn. We leave Qunu and go to the place where we're going to be circumcised and stay for three weeks before we return to the village as men. We arrive and walk to the kraal where we meet the *ingcibi* who will perform the ritual, and I know shit is about to get real.

"Take off your clothes."

Okay. We do that, like snakes shedding our skin, transforming into something elemental and raw. I am told to sit on a rock while the holy man who'll be with us throughout the whole ordeal explains everything that's about to happen and everything that's expected of us in the process. He directs us to enter the kraal, which is where the animals usually stay at night. I walk barefoot across the dirt and cow dung floor and sit on the rock, willing myself to remain perfectly still, listening as the *ingcibi* progresses down the row toward me with an assistant carrying his *assegai*—the sharp spears that will be used. He has more than one, because each initiate requires a fresh blade. My heart is pounding in my chest. I force myself to breathe slow, regulated breaths, just as the Old Man instructed me, knees separated, locked at a ninety-degree angle.

Now the *ingcibi* steps into position.

"Look to the East!"

I turn my face to the East. I feel the searing stroke of the blade. A sickening shiver shoots down my spine, followed by a shockwave of agony and adrenaline. Involuntarily, I cough twice, and then I turn my face to the West and bellow.

"Ndiyindoda! Ndiyindoda! Ndiyindoda!"

The *ingcibi* moves on to the next chap, leaving me suspended in a blinding aura of pain unlike anything I've ever experienced or could have been remotely prepared for.

I am a man.

Despite the intense heat in the kraal, gut-deep trembling overtakes me. The body's natural shock response.

I am a man.

I'm like a tightrope walker. I dare not look down. I have to look down. I see blood dripping from my manhood.

I am a man.

After he finishes with the last guy, the *ingcibi* washes his hands. He comes to me with a plant and a goatskin strap. He ties my piece with it, sort of like a bandage. Someone places a blanket around my shoulders. A

domed hut called an *iboma* has been built by the vil-
lagers to accommodate the initiates during the rest of
the ritual. Thorny branches are laid out on the ground
all around it, leaving a narrow path to the single doorway. Someone leads me to the *iboma*, and I gingerly sit
down, trying to breathe. Other than the bandage-like
thing and a strap around my waist, I am naked. During
this transition period, I am neither boy nor man; I am
an animal. We are all animals. God is an animal.

The first day, there's not a lot of conversation. We
go around the room and introduce ourselves, giving our
clan name, and where we're from. When it's my turn,
I say, *"Madiba. Yem-Yem uSpicho, Vele-bam-bestele.
Igama lam lesfana ngu-Ndaba."* (My name is Ndaba.)
"Ndisuka eQunu." (I'm from Qunu.) *"Inkosiyam ngu-
Nokwanele."* (My chief is Nokwanele.)

I listen carefully, trying to memorize the names of
everyone in the circle. For seven days, I'll remain with
my fellow initiates in the *iboma*. For obvious reasons,
we're not given water or anything else to drink. We
eat only a stiff mash of boiled maize. We sleep on the
ground with only the blanket, and you can't sleep laid
out straight or on your side; you sleep on your back with
your knees elevated. I dream strange dreams and wake
up frequently, because every time I move the slightest
bit, a bolt of agony shoots through my midsection. I lie

on the ground thinking, *This is hell. My father must hate me to put me through this torture. How dare they do this to me? This is madness.*

The second day, someone comes to show us how to dress the wound with fresh leaves called *isicwe*. It has tiny hairs on it that stick to the wound, so you can imagine when it's time to change it, removing it is no simple task. Every inch is agony, and then a few minutes later, you have to put on another one. *Yeesh*. They tell us we must do this several times a day, no matter how painful it is, and it is incredibly painful. This will continue for weeks until the wound is fully healed.

The next day, we cover our faces and bodies with white clay and sit like ghosts in the *iboma*. My stomach aches with hunger. I'm grateful to see that some *amasi* has been added to the maize, but I'm so thirsty, the inside of my mouth feels like an old shoe. The thirst is crazy-making. I tell myself, *Don't think about water. Don't think about water. Don't think about Beyoncé. Don't think about Holyfield's scabby ear or P. Diddy's dance moves or Ms. Dynamite from London town.*

The seventh day, I'm so weak with hunger and thirst, I can hardly find strength to slather myself with the white clay that will protect my skin when I go outside, and I am so freaking ready to go outside. I smell goat roasting out there. More than anything, I just want to get my hands on some of that. And water. That first swig of cold water is everything—grace, life, courage, God— but they tell us, "Don't drink too much! Remember, it has to come out somewhere, and you know what that means. Pain!"

The second week, we're allowed to drink alcohol and smoke some weed, which is a tremendous relief. You have to pay for it, so the *khanki*, the elders looking after you, bring money.

Over the following weeks, we smear ourselves with white clay every morning before leaving the *iboma*. It feels good to walk out into the bush, breathing fresh air, using a machete to gather firewood. We also gather the leaves for the dressing, which we must continue to apply diligently, but not as often, because the wounds are healing remarkably fast. We spend time hanging out, talking about home and school and women. At some point, we must be "hit by the wind," which means you get naked and let the wind—okay, too much information. It's therapeutic. Let's leave it at that.

One might think that a crew of guys who'd grown up with video games and computers would get bored sitting there day after day, but for me at least, that's not the case. As the weeks go by, we learn songs about manhood, about life, about women. There's one about writing a letter to a lover and one called *"Isipringi Seb-hedi"* ("Springs of the Bed") that tells a story about women and girls and *this woman is gonna kill me, I love her, she's amazing* and so forth. We learn a sort of secret language—different words for chair, food, water, whatever—and we hear stories about our ancestors. Days pass, and the smell is indescribable because we are twenty animals in the *iboma* and we're not able to bathe or shower.

After three weeks, we go to the river to wash ourselves, walking as a group, wrapped in our blankets, carrying sticks, soap, and limestone. We grind the limestone on the river rocks until it becomes a viscous white paste, and we smear it on our bodies from head to toe, covering the brown skin that makes us human. We stay that way until the last three days, when the ritual is taken to yet another level. We return to our village—I and the two others of my clan—and the next night, we dance with our sisters. You're naked except for the blanket tied around your middle, and you have to dance, holding a stick above your head. The sisters and brothers and cousins come with needles, and they prick you with the needle every now and then. I can only guess at the purpose of this. If you think about it, some symbology is bound to emerge, but in the moment, you're just trying to avoid getting jabbed. You dance until you're exhausted and sweating, and when the girls get tired of it, they leave.

The final night is a huge celebration with food and brandy and a traditional beer we make ourselves and drink out of clay pot or tin jug. You drink and pass it around. All the guys in the village have heard and are like, "Hey, those guys are back, and one of them is a Mandela!" So they want to inspect the situation and make sure that the deed has been properly done. They want to see that wound and verify that it's the real deal. There are different styles of cut—small, middle, hand-bag (loosely translated from the traditional names)—so they want to see which one you got. What can we do? We show them, and they're duly impressed. One guy is so enthusiastic, he shows me his.

"Yes, you have a very good cut," he says. "See, mine was done seven years ago, and you can see that it didn't heal properly."

They have to show respect now. You've earned all the privileges of being a man. You feel like a man. Iron Man! Untouchable. A god. You have done your family proud. Pass the beer pot! You experience this intense rush of power, so sometimes guys take it into their heads to disrespect their parents. They become problems at home. This is why it's important to end the ritual with long conversational sessions. Our elders come to visit us—patriarchs, uncles, older brothers, and cousins—to share their wisdom and teach us the customs and traditions, reminding us that it will be our responsibility to pass all this on to our children. They remind us to respect our mothers and aunties, because a real man respects his mama. A real man helps out at home and contributes to the family's happiness. A real man is not useless in his home or community. He has power and he uses it to add value to his surroundings.

"You're a man now," says Madiba. He sits in his chair, super chill and glad to be here. "You must understand that you will be one of the men in our home. It's up to you to take care of the home and look after the women and children. Make us proud. We are from the royal house of the Thembus. We are the fourth house. Our role is to be mediators." He talks to me for a long time about getting in touch with my ancestors and knowing my roots. Respecting where I come from. Recognizing what I am. He tells me stories about his own going to the mountain, and we compare notes on our experiences.

"In that time," says the Old Man, "part of the ritual was that we must steal a pig, slaughter it, and eat the whole thing the night before we went in. This was someone's pig in the community, but we did as we were told—as we were guided by ritual. I tempted the pig out of the kraal with the sap left over in the bottom of a beer tin. He came out to eat, and we all descended on him. We dug a pit near the *iboma* and roasted it. We ate that pig, and then we were prepared to go hungry for a week."

The final step of *Ukwaluka* is "crossing the river." You get in the water and scrub all that white stuff off your body, so when you go to meet up with your family, you are clean and wrapped in a blanket called an *i-ruggy*. You don't wear your own clothes again until it's all over and you're ready to begin your life as a man among them.

The celebration was a proud moment for our family and lasted the whole weekend. Parents, grandparents, aunts, and uncles offered words of encouragement and wisdom to me and my cousins. When we all sat down at the big table to eat dinner, my granddad said, "Are you good, Ndaba? Are you healthy?" I was surprised to hear him speaking isiXhosa. He hardly ever spoke to me in isiXhosa. It was always English. But he spoke to me in isiXhosa now, acknowledging my manhood.

"Yes, Granddad, I'm fine."

"Good. Good. You're a man now, Ndaba. You've done well."

"Thank you, Granddad."

"Ndaba, what do you think about the cows?" he asked. "Do you know how many there are? You're an adult now. You'll have to stay current on the business of the farm."

"I will, Granddad. Absolutely."

It made me feel older, wiser, and maybe even a bit taller. We danced and drank and danced and ate and drank more and then went back to dancing. Later, we went into the village to hang out with the other men, young and old, who always gather at someone's house to drink. Everyone was happy to see us. Madiba was glad to come out into the community to spend time with them.

The next morning, the Old Man asked me to fetch his newspapers. Again I was surprised, because one of the security people usually brought the papers to him, and if I passed by, he'd motion me to sit down. This was new. We were doing this together. I brought the papers, and we read them all, front to back, conversing about events and issues. Instead of feeding me bits of news like a mama bird feeds a hatchling, he allowed me to digest it for myself, and then asked my opinion about it. He expected critical thinking and welcomed civilized disagreements rather than rote learning and head nodding. I can look back now and see that this is where we turned a page in our relationship. From the time I was a kid, I knew I could depend on him. This is when he knew he could depend on me.

It's hard to encompass—and it wouldn't be appropriate for me to describe it all here—the depth and breadth of tradition conveyed throughout the ritual weeks. You connect with your spirituality and heritage. Who are you? What family do you represent? Which village do you come from? You have an obligation to abide by the code of your people and endure the pain like a man. You come to understand who you are, from a cultural point of view, and it makes you feel stronger, more confident.

Pierre Teilhard de Chardin, a French paleontologist and Jesuit priest, said, "We are not human beings having a spiritual experience; we are spiritual beings having a human experience." As I crossed the river, I experienced a convergence of the two. I was essentially animal, essentially spirit, uniquely myself. I was firmly tethered to my ancestors, and in turn, I tethered them to the future.

My birth name was Thembekile: "the trusted one."

My manhood name is Zwelijika: "the world is changing."

10

Indlu enkulu ifuna.

"A great house needs a strong broom."

One of the strangest stories I heard when I was growing up is The Story of Nongqawuse's Prophesy. This young girl returns from the river one day and tells the people of her village, "Two ancestors visited me and told me that all the dead will rise again." Folks were like, "Awesome!" They would get to see their loved ones again, and this was very cool. But in order for the Big Day to happen, she said, the people must slaughter all their cattle, dig up their grain, and basically destroy and rebuild everything—huts, kraals, whatever—all gone. Now a lot of folks were like, "Homey don't play dat," but a lot of others bought into it and started putting on the pressure to participate. Even the king and most of the chiefs got all caught up in this idea that the dead Xhosa nations would come up out of the sea, bringing new cattle, sheep, and chickens, and—key point here—drive out the white invaders. They believed in a golden age when there would be no more disease or sorrow. They slaughtered their cattle, and when the Big Day came and went without an army of ancestors rising from the sea, rather than saying, "Hmm, perhaps this was not a good idea," they blamed unbelievers who had refused to slaughter their cattle. Not surprisingly, many of the unbelievers and their cattle were slaughtered forthwith, and the farms they had protected were plundered. A famine ensued. Hunger and desperation swept across the cape. An estimated forty thousand Xhosa people died.

The strangest thing about this story is that it happened. Google Nongqawuse, and you'll see a haunting photograph of this strange girl who led the Xhosa people into a hell of their own making in 1856. Questions still swirl around this catastrophic incident, and the most compelling one is, *"Why?"* But isn't that always the most compelling question?

Through the lens of political history, you see many such incidents throughout the world, going back centuries. Certain elements stand in common: A society-wide state of purposeful blindness is disguised as religious fervor. Hate that already existed on some level is weaponized. And then there's the real motor on it: Someone stands ready to take advantage of the situation to gain power, money, or both. In the case of the cattle killings prompted by Nongqawuse's prophesy, the colonial government responded to widespread famine with a "recruitment program" that offered starving people the opportunity to sell themselves into slavery. In the case of America's Salem Witch Trials, wealthy neighbors took the land of elderly women being tortured and put to death. In the case of the AIDS pandemic, power struggles, pharmaceutical trademarks, conservative religion, racism, homophobia, ignorance, and willful indifference have all played their parts. If you want to read a dense but riveting book about how the AIDS epidemic started, read *And the Band Played On* by Randy Shilts. The title refers to the orchestra that played on the deck of the *Titanic* as the ship sank and most of her passengers drowned.

I can't condemn the people who chose for so long to

live in denial about the hard realities of AIDS in South Africa and the rest of the world. I was one of them. While my mother was dying, I couldn't make room in my mind for the idea that she had HIV until someone basically punched me in the face with the flatly stated truth. And even after that experience, I was unwilling to make the obvious connections when my dad started to get sick. I knew that he had been in and out of hospital—I had driven him there myself on more than one occasion—but I kept telling myself, "People get sick. It's no big deal." He'd come out of the hospital and get back to work. I was busy with school and focused on my studies.

The year after I went to the mountain, I got an apartment near the university in Pretoria. I spent every weekend at home with my grandfather and popped in as often as I could during the week for lunch or dinner or just to say, "Hey, Granddad, how are you doing?" I was finally allowed to invite a girl to dinner. As we sat down to eat, the Old Man said, "So, young lady, did you propose to my grandson?" This was his line, it turns out. He used it on a number of occasions. I guess he enjoyed seeing the looks on their faces.

I liked this easier dynamic between my granddad and me, but his age was beginning to show. He maintained his inflexible daily routine: Wake up early in the morning. Walk and exercise. Breakfast. Newspapers.

But now instead of going off to the office, he relaxed in the lounge and often took a nap. He liked it when people came for lunch, and after lunch most days, he watched National Geographic or sports until it was time for afternoon tea, which often included visitors. He traveled sometimes for public appearances, but it seemed to take a lot out of him in a way I wasn't quite ready for. Honestly, I worried more about him than I worried about my dad. He and my father saw each other now and then, and the Old Man certainly never voiced any concerns to me, but I do recall one day when we were sitting together at the table and he told me about how his own father died.

"I was nine years old," he said. "My father spent one week with each of his wives—four wives, four weeks— so once a month, he came to us. Only this particular day, he came to my mother's hut when he was not scheduled. I came home and found him in a terrible state, coughing, coughing, coughing. He stayed with us for several days. His younger wife came to help my mother care for him. One night, he called for his pipe, and my mother didn't want to give it to him. She said, 'No. Clearly, he has some disease of the lungs. He shouldn't smoke.' I'm certain she was correct, but my father didn't go to any doctor. He had no use for that. He wanted his pipe. He was quite insistent. Kept yelling, 'Bring me my pipe!'

No one in the house was sleeping, because he was getting quite aggravated. So the young wife filled his pipe with tobacco and brought it to him. Smoking calmed him down. He smoked for a while, and then he died, the pipe was in his hand, still lit. I could smell the tobacco in the air."

I listened to the story, though I wasn't sure why he felt the need to tell it to me at that moment. I didn't give it a lot of thought. The Old Man was full of stories.

"When my father died," he said, "I was not prepared for that level of grief."

"But how could you be, Granddad? You were just a little boy."

"Even after I became a man, I looked for him inside myself."

I glanced at my watch. "Granddad, I need to get back to school."

"Yes. Good. Very good." He stood up to walk me to the door. "I'm very proud of you, Ndaba. Your father is very proud of you as well."

I was already halfway out to my car, calling "goodbye" over my shoulder, because I had things to do, people to see, exams to write, holidays to enjoy. I was living the busy life of a student who's finally found his direction and is flying through every day, full speed ahead. As the year went by, I noticed that my dad was losing weight. He became painfully thin, and I still kept telling myself it was just normal stuff. He still kept telling me, "Oh, I'm fine. Don't sweat it. It'll be fine."

In December 2004, my dad went into the hospital, and it was very clearly not going to be fine. Mandla finally got frustrated with my unwillingness to face the truth.

"Our father has HIV/AIDS," he said bluntly. "He gave it to your mom. How do you think she got it?"

I couldn't believe I was standing in the same hospital hallway, absorbing the same throat punch I'd gotten from my mother's doctor two years earlier. I was no more prepared for it in this moment than I was back then. I was gutted. Again. I was angry with the people who didn't trust me with the truth and angry with myself for failing to figure it out on my own. I was smart enough to make the connection; I just didn't want to believe it. I *chose* to be blind to what was happening, because I didn't want him to die. I wasn't ready to be cast adrift again.

But beyond all that, I wasn't ready or willing to live with another lie, and I knew that the public relations people would be all over us, providing us with carefully chosen words to say, asking for privacy in our time of grief, brushing aside ugly rumors. To hell with all of them. It was Mbuso and Andile I cared about.

They were twelve and nine at the time. As my father lay dying, I made the heartbreaking discovery that Auntie Maki had known for quite some time about my dad's HIV status and chose not to tell the rest of the family. I felt the same surge of anger I felt when I found out my mother had kept the truth from me.

I kept insisting, "We have to tell Mbuso and Andile. This isn't right."

"No," she said. "They don't have to know."

"Auntie, it's going to be on international television. Even if you could somehow keep them from seeing it, the other kids at school—kids are animals. It's not their fault. They're just naturally going to repeat what they hear at home."

"They're children. They can't understand."

"Which is exactly why someone who cares about them should sit them down and explain it! You can say it was pneumonia—make up whatever story and justify it—but people are speculating. They're not stupid. And if you keep on denying it, you're complicit in the stigma that's killing him."

"Oh, don't put that on me! I do what's right for my family. You don't think this family has given enough? Suffered enough? Now we're responsible for the world?"

We went back and forth, exhausted by sadness, arguing in circles. It was a horrible time for everyone. A hopeless situation. I was losing my father. Madiba was losing his son. Auntie Maki was losing her brother. Each of us was going through such turmoil in our own heart, it was hard to reach out to each other. Any discussion of what anyone was going to say or not say—this was all moot. We are a patriarchal people. My grandfather would tell us what we were or were not going to say, and although he was an outspoken advocate for HIV/ AIDS funding and awareness, it seemed to me that this openness about AIDS applied only to other families, not the Mandelas. I'd gotten that message when my mother died. I didn't expect anything different now, and although I didn't always agree with the Old Man, I trusted him to decide what was best for the family. He was going through the hell of losing a son for the second time, and I was prepared to support him.

At the end of December, I spent my twenty-second birthday sitting with my dad, trying to smile and converse with him as he hacked and rasped. He fought the need to doze. I fought to keep down the memories of going through this same situation with my mom.

The traditional Xhosa belief is that, when a person dies, their spirit lingers in the room for a time. There were times that he laid so still, and his breath was so shallow, I couldn't tell if his spirit was just inside or just beyond his fragile skin. During that last month, the Old

Man spent many days at the hospital. Sometimes I could hear them talking quietly, even laughing, but most of the time, it seemed to me that they were just sitting there together.

My father, Makgatho Lewanika Mandela, died January 6, 2005. He was one of over five million South Africans who were infected with HIV at the time. 1.6 million South Africans had already died.

We left the hospital, and it seemed like my granddad had aged forty years on the way to the car. He leaned heavily on his walking stick, his shoulders sagging, his gait unsteady. Reporters and paparazzi swarmed forward, shouting questions at Madiba as we tried to help him into the car. The Old Man turned to them for a moment. He had tears in his eyes. His voice was shaky. He said, "My son was an attorney by profession, and he was actually admitted as an attorney by the Judge President of this province, which was a great honor. Beyond that, I've nothing to say."

That afternoon, the family gathered at our house in Houghton. Madiba had called a press conference for later that day, and he wanted us all to be there. Everyone was very emotional. Everyone had a different opinion about what should be said. I didn't even look up to see who was talking. I'd heard it all before.

"It's no one's business—our private family matters."

I was familiar with the mental gymnastics people practiced in order to avoid the truth.

"People don't die of HIV. It weakens them. AIDS kills your immune system."

"That's true. It's pneumonia that kills you. Or TB. We can actually say TB."

"*No!*" the Old Man barked, and the room fell silent. "We will not say that. We will say that HIV/AIDS killed him. Let's stop beating around the bush. We need to fight the stigma, not facilitate it. We should give publicity to HIV/AIDS and not hide it. Because the only way of making it appear to be a normal illness—like TB, like cancer—is to come out and say it. Somebody has died because of HIV. If we refuse to say it, people will never stop regarding it as something extraordinary."

The reporters had already gathered in the garden behind the house, maneuvering for camera angles and piling microphones on a coffee table that had been set in front of two side chairs near the flowering hedges. Bees buzzed in and out of the pale pink blossoms, and Madiba impatiently waved one away from his face as Graça helped him to his chair and sat next to him. My brothers and I stood behind Madiba, and the rest of the family gathered around us, unified, dignified, eyes forward, jaws set hard. The clicking of the cameras and the buzzing of the bees vibrated inside my head. This was the last place in the world I wanted to be at that moment. I was nervous. Glad to have my family around me. Grateful to know that we were doing the right thing. I would be able to talk about my father and not feel like a coward.

My grandfather's face was etched with sorrow, but he showed very little emotion. He spoke in the firm, measured way he always spoke. He began with a few words about "46664" and the work of the Nelson Mandela Foundation. Then he said, "I had no idea when I started this campaign three years ago that it would also affect a member of my family. I was stating a general principal that we must not hide the cause of death of our respective family. Because that is the only way in which we can make people understand that HIV is an ordinary illness. And that's why we've called you today. To announce that my son has died of AIDS. It is a very bad reflection indeed on the members of a family that they themselves should not come out and say bravely, 'A member of my family has died of AIDS.' That is why we took the initiative to say that a member of our family has died. In this particular case, my son."

Moments later, the firestorm response hit the Internet and television news. Nelson Mandela's son had died of HIV/AIDS. There was no way to open a newspaper or turn on a TV without being confronted by the fact that our nation and the world was being ravaged by this disease. Madiba was proud of his son, the attorney, Makgatho Lewanika Mandela. He was not ashamed, and he was no longer willing to be complicit in the shame of others. And this changed things. As you read this, the world has changed—maybe not enough, certainly not fast enough—but something did shift that day. It was a groundbreaking moment. This was the first time a prominent South African family had openly acknowledged that a family member had died of HIV/AIDS. It's impossible to overstate what this meant to the millions of people who lived in fear of seeking help or disclosing their HIV status and to the millions more people who loved them.

We took my father to Qunu and buried him with all the rites and traditions of his people. During the funeral, I sat stoically between Graça and Auntie Maki, aching with loss, reminding myself, *I endure, I endure.* A man endures.

In 1974 Robben Island inmate #46664 wrote to his son: "It's not easy to write to a person who hardly ever replies." It pains me to say that, throughout much of my life, I knew exactly how the prisoner felt. Disconnected. Out of the loop. I loved my father, and I know he loved me, and oddly enough, I actually feel closer to him now than I did when I was a kid. I suppose that's because I am now the age that he was when my first memories of him were formed. We were a relatively happy little family in Cofimvaba, and he managed my grandmother's grocery store. He was a good man. He worked his ass off. He was humble. He wasn't always present in my life—not the way I wanted him to be—but he opened the door for other father figures who shaped my life and ideals. My grandfather, first and foremost, Kweku's father, my uncle Kwame, Walter Sisulu, and many others. My dad was proud of me. Even though I hadn't quite found my best self yet, I was on the right track. I think he passed away knowing I'd be all right, and I hope that eased the way for his lingering spirit.

His death lit a fire under my grandfather's desire to make HIV/AIDS the last great fight of his life, so I'd like to think that whatever lives have been saved or suffering eased since that time and in the future—that this, in a way, is my father's gift. Throughout his presidency, the cause of HIV/AIDS was close to Madiba's heart, because he couldn't bear to see his people suffering—especially the little children—but the challenges and affairs of state during those years were overwhelmingly directed toward transforming the colonial government into a democracy and the divided people into one nation. Now he had the freedom to choose how he spent his time and the last of his energy.

NDABA MANDELA

The week after the funeral in Qunu, the Old Man called another press conference. That deep sorrow was still etched in the lines around his eyes, but he made an attempt to joke with the assembled press.

"What I have come to do here this morning is to make an appeal, more than an announcement. I'm turning eighty-six in a few weeks' time, and that is a longer life than most people are granted. . . . I am confident that nobody present here today will accuse me of selfishness if I asked to spend time while I'm still in good health with my family, my friends, and also with myself."

The journalists laughed a little uncertainly, as if they didn't quite know where he was going with this train of thought.

"When I told one of my advisors a few months ago that I wanted to retire, he growled at me, 'Goat! You are retired!' If that really is the case, then I should say I now announce that I am retiring from retirement."

11

Akukho rhamncwa elingagqumiyo
emngxumeni walo.

"There is no beast that does not roar in its own den."

Not long after Madiba left office, Richard Branson and Peter Gabriel came to him and Graça with the idea of forming a small group of people who might direct the wisdom of their years and benefit of their experience to resolving conflicts and solving problems such as climate change and the global AIDS pandemic. It took them a few years to convince the Old Man. His initial response was, "I don't know if the rest of the world wants a lot of old-timers involved." They made the compelling argument that, while trust in institutions and governments was failing, certain people maintained a level of moral authority. When these people spoke, people believed them. When they acted, people trusted that it was free of agenda, for the good of all.

At the official launch of The Elders in Johannesburg on July 18, 2007, my granddad's eighty-ninth birthday, he said: "Let us call them Global Elders, not because of their age, but because of their individual and collective wisdom. This group derives its strength not from political, economic, or military power, but from the independence and integrity of those who are here. They do not have careers to build, elections to win, constituencies to please. They can talk to anyone they please, and are free to follow paths they deem right, even if hugely unpopular."

The original Elders were men and women of varied race and creed, including Archbishop Desmond Tutu, former US president Jimmy Carter, former Irish president Mary Robinson, and Kofi Annan.

"Using their collective experience," said Madiba, "their moral courage and their ability to rise above the parochial concerns of nation, race, and creed, they can help make our planet a more peaceful, healthy, and equitable place to live." He called on The Elders and all those gathered in the auditorium to "support courage where there is fear, foster agreement where there is conflict, and inspire hope where there is despair."

I thought this was an amazing idea. I was hip-deep in my studies, working toward my degree in international relations and political science, developing my own ideas about human rights and history, and coming to the conclusion that the problems of the next generation were going to be very different from the challenges faced by our parents and grandparents.

I asked my granddad, "On a practical level, what does it take to effect this grand scale of change they're talking about? Without political power, are they limited to an advisory sort of capacity, or can they actually do something?"

"These esteemed friends of mine have a long history of doing the things they set out to do," he said. "I'm certain that if Tutu has anything to do with it, they will insist on assuming the spirit of *ubuntu*."

Ubuntu is, in the Old Man's words, "that profound African sense that we are human only through the humanity of other beings." One would like to think that this would be foundational to the idea of politics—a word that comes from the Greek *politikos*, "citizenship"—but sometimes it's a struggle to connect the two, even for Nelson Mandela, but in the years following my father's death, his work made a noticeable shift toward social and cultural issues. He was keenly interested in the mindset of young people and enjoyed long conversations with me and his other grandchildren, but he was not as predictable as he was when I was a kid.

He still cared about protocol, but I recall one occasion when he and Graça and I were in Europe at a dinner hosted by members of a royal family, and I was appalled to see two people at our table light up cigarettes as soon as they sat down next to my granddad. They sat there chain-smoking one cigarette after another throughout the entire evening. This was the sort of thing that would have irritated him mightily in years past, but he sat chatting happily with them as they blazed through two packs each.

I hated the conclusion that nudged at the back of my mind: *He's getting really old.*

During my last year at the university, I tried to spend as much time as possible at home. I found myself worrying about the Old Man, feeling protective of him, questioning the energy he devoted to so many causes and occasions that required him to travel. I went with him when it was possible, but most of the time, I was concentrating on school—which is what he wanted me to do anyway—so it was good to know that Graça was there for him. As I came to understand more about the cattle business and the nonprofit world, I began developing my own opinions about these institutions, and though we didn't always agree, he always wanted to hear what I had to say.

One day we were talking about someone with whom he'd done business, and I commented that this person struck me as a bit of a snake.

"A snake?" the Old Man said, surprised at my choice of words. "But you know he and I have been friends for many years, and we have never had a quarrel. Not a single quarrel!"

"Then something's off," I said. "No two people agree 100 percent, Granddad. Somebody in that relationship is not being real, and I know that ain't you."

He digested that and nodded. "That is true. A common feature shared by Sisulu and Kathrada—an essential part of our friendship—they never hesitated to tell me that I was wrong. I value that very much. The true friend is the mirror in which you accurately see yourself."

I was grateful to have the Old Man be that mirror for me, and it meant a lot to me to see that I'd begun to repair his trust in me. That trust continued to grow over the years, and I never took it for granted. One day during the last year of his life, Mama Xoli called me to the kitchen and said, "Ndaba, please go up to your grandfather's room." She told me she'd seen three close associates go into Madiba's room. "I don't have a good feeling about this," said Mama Xoli. I didn't either. My granddad had gotten very frail. He and Graça slept in separate rooms, but a nurse was always with him— wo nurses most of the time— and when I went upstairs, the nurse was nowhere to be seen. My granddad was in bed, and the three of them stood over him. He had a pen in his hand and a paper in front of him.

"*Yintoni le*?" I said in isiXhosa. ("What is this?")

"Ndaba, your grandpa is getting very old, and the bank is starting to question his signature." There was a long explanation about how his hands were shaky so the signature was not as crisp as it should be. The punchline was that this was a power of attorney document he was signing, handing over access to his bank accounts. The pen was nudged in his hand and they said, "It's okay, Madiba. We've explained it to Ndaba. You can sign now."

The Old Man looked up at me, and I said, "*Unga linge ubhale lo-phepha.*" ("Do not sign that paper.") It made me uncomfortable that no family member was included in this arrangement.

"Why are you not speaking English?" one of them asked.

"He's my grandfather," I said. "Why wouldn't I speak our language?"

"What are you saying?"

"That's between my granddad and myself."

There was some additional back and forth, pleading with him to sign, demanding to know what I was saying to him, but the upshot was that he refused to sign, and after a while, they got frustrated and left. I called Aunt Maki and asked her what she thought of all this. She told me to get the paper so she could see it, and I managed to do that. The next day, a different version was drafted to include Madiba's daughters. And Aunt Maki was satisfied with that.

For my part, this moment made me realize that my granddad needed me to stay close by. I'm not saying that there were any nefarious dealings going on or accusing anyone of wrongdoing, but for me, the takeaway from all this was that trust is fragile, and family is strong. At the end of his life, when he was at his most vulnerable, the Old Man knew I had his back the same way he had always had mine. At the end of his life, when he was at his most vulnerable, the Old Man knew I had his back the same way he had always had mine.

In December 2008, I wrote my final exams. The results came back in January, and when I showed them to the Old Man, he was pleased, which was a good feeling. He smiled broadly and offered me his palm to slap.

"You got your degree," he said.

"Graduation's in April," I said. "Will you come?"

"Of course! Absolutely. Speak with the security people. Make the arrangement."

As the date approached, I got everything set with security. Everything nice and ready. I went and picked up my gown. Does it fit? Yes. Good. Everything's cool.

On graduation day, I hopped out of the car first and went to where I was supposed to go, sitting with the rest of the graduating class. I had reserved seats for my granddad, Graça, and Mandla, but the Old Man had waived the suggestion of a whole reserved section because he didn't want any other parents to be prevented from attending.

So finally people were all in their places. For security reasons, Madiba had to come in last, and when he came in, the place erupted in great joy. Everybody stood up, cheering, so happy to see him. "Mandela's here! Madiba! Madiba!" People lost themselves in that moment.

The ceremony commenced. I waited for my name to be called. I had thought a lot about what I wanted to do when I went out on the stage. Everybody had their own thing. I had settled on a Black Power sign—the symbol for the ANC, Black Unity, Black Power. Back in the day, Madiba would hold his fist in the air and shout, *"Amandla!"* ("The power!") And all the people would all shout back, *"Ngawethu!"* ("It is ours!") So that was my plan.

I heard my name, and I choked. I don't know what happened. It was like one minute, I was totally there, and the next minute, they called my name, and I froze. It was only a fraction of a second, but it felt like a lifetime. I looked out over the crowd and saw my grandfather. The look on his face was absolute pride, absolute happiness, this beautiful smile about five kilometers wide. It was as though every memory, every moment of my life uploaded to my spine—from the *thok! thok!* of the tear gas cannon to the ripe heat of the *iboma*. I smiled back at the Old Man and did a modest fist pump, just to say *thank you*. And then I walked across the stage, an educated man, and claimed this future for which my grandfather had fought and suffered.

Afterward, I made my way over to Madiba and Graça outside, taking my time, because I always tend to hang back from the cameras. There was no advance announcement that Madiba would be there, but a few industrious paparazzi had figured out that he probably would. The security detail held them at a reasonable distance, but a lot of students and family members wanted to get autographs and pictures with Madiba.

"Good to see you." He'd offer his hand as they approached. "I'm Nelson Mandela."

As we walked to the car, I teased him about that. "You really think you need to introduce yourself?"

"I don't presume," he said. "On one occasion in the Caribbean, a gentleman and his wife passed by me on the sidewalk. The gentleman says, 'Darling, look, it's Mr. Mandela! Mr. Mandela!' She said to me, 'Oh, what are you famous for?' I did not know how to answer that question."

I laughed, and he reached over to grasp my forearm.

"Well done, Ndaba."

"Thanks, Granddad."

"You should be very proud of yourself."

I thought about it and decided I was. I had achieved this goal that meant so much to him, but at the end of the day, I had done it for myself—and of course, that is what he wanted for me all along.

"So now what are you going to do?" he asked.

"Go look for a job."

"Good, good," said the Old Man. "First, we'll have lunch."

✿   ✿   ✿

ONCE UPON A TIME, a magic tree grew up so tall with branches so wide it cast a shadow over an entire village. The sun was obstructed, crops couldn't grow, and people got cold and hungry, so the chief sends his tallest, strongest man out to cut the tree down. But a bird who lives at the very top of the tree starts singing, *"This tree belongs to me! This tree belongs to me!"* The guy hears this enchanted song, and he's paralyzed—utterly unable to swing the axe. The chief sends the second tallest man, the third, fourth, and so on. Same thing. The enchanted song stops every big man in his tracks. Meanwhile, the people of the village are shivering and starving.

"Send your children to cut the tree down," says a wise old lady.

The chief thinks she's crazy. "How could my little children cut down a tree that can't be felled by these tall men?"

But he's desperate, so he sends out his little son and daughter, and very soon the tree comes crashing down. The children are not so tall, you see. They're closer to the ground, so they can't hear the bird, and the enchanted song has no power over them.

I hope when kids hear that story, they stop and think about the power that rests in their hands.

"It is up to the youth," Madiba said, "to decisively and finally break our society out of the constricting and divisive definitions of our past." The keyword in that statement, I think, is *definitions*. While the generation before us was defined by apartheid, defined by Bantu education, defined by poverty, my generation and our little brothers and sisters, the born frees, are living the new lexicon. We speak the streamlined language of technology, and we're creating the culture we want to live in.

I graduated college with all these ideas rolling around in my head. For years, Kweku and I had been brainstorming ways to elevate Africa in the eyes of the world and, more important, in the eyes of Africans themselves. Now we started talking in concrete terms about this far-reaching dream, which was nothing less than a full-on African renaissance, a cultural revolution, harnessing the full powers of education, entrepreneurship, social media, music, film, television, fashion, podcasts—all the technology that brings millennials together—infused with Africa's ancient creative soul. Inspired by the past and stoked about the future, we created a foundation called Africa Rising.

We got the ball rolling with an informal meetup. We just called a few friends and invited them to tell their friends. We hoped that maybe ten people would come. Twenty-five people showed up. It was like an arc of electricity. I don't know why it surprised me. Of course, Kweku and I weren't the only ones who'd been having these thoughts. Youth all over Africa, no matter what they were interested in—sports, music, business, fashion—were all coming to the same realization we had come to. They had dreams and ideas, and they wanted opportunities and access that would allow them to make all their dreams reality. We stood there in this room full of entrepreneurs, creative thinkers, changemakers, and artists, and we knew something significant was happening. A period of transformation had already begun.

Kweku and I went to our granddad and asked him to act as honorary trustee, knowing that we would face the same slow pitch that Branson and Gabriel had to work through. The Old Man wasn't going to sign off on it just because he loved us. We had a memorized mission statement, answers to logistical questions, and a bulleted list of solid objectives.

I told my granddad, "Our goal is to break down the misconceptions the world has about Africa—change that image that automatically pops into their heads—in order to uplift the pride, dignity, and confidence of young Africans. It has to start here. And not like another NGO. We have to empower the youth through education, entrepreneurship, technology—all that—but we also have to lift their pride and confidence so they can say, 'I'm an African. I know what it means to be an African, and I'm proud of it.' We have to work together and do it for our own people. There is no Asia or Europe or America that will create a prosperous Africa."

He listened, nodded. "Start how?"

"Practical first steps," I said. "Education. HIV/ AIDS screening. Social media campaigns. We cultivate a new generation of African leaders, aggressively develop programs for high schoolers and college students. We participate in festivals and conferences. We go everywhere we can go, talk to everybody we can talk to. We speak out when we see something messed up, and when we see something good, we lift it up to inspire people. Granddad, think about how differently all that 1960s stuff would have gone down if you'd had social media, podcasts—all the power of the people magnified times two hundred million. That's what we have right here in our hands. We could literally achieve *anything*."

All my life, my grandfather never pushed me to do one thing or another in specific. His reaction, positive or negative, was always measured. He never got super enthusiastic, like, "Oh, boy! Yes! And you could also do this or that or this other thing." He'd nod and offer a circumspect, "Good. Very good." This time was no different, but he did agree to become an honorary trustee.

"Write up a letter," he said. "I'll go over it."

I wrote the letter, and we went back and forth a bit editing it. When he signed it, he said, "You must ask Thabo Mbeki what he thinks of these things. He knows young people much better than me."

I doubted this was true, but I remembered what my granddad said about that fearless mirror your true friends will hold up for you, and I knew Kweku and I could trust President Mbeki to give an honest opinion.

I fell into a pattern that one might call "responsible rebellion." I was determined to make a way for myself independent of Madiba's footsteps, but I felt a deep sense of responsibility to him and to the name Mandela. I didn't just go on impulse anymore; I thought about things before I made a statement or took action. While Kweku and I continued laying the foundation for Africa Rising, I worked at the Japanese embassy during the day and spent my evenings either doing research on my laptop or hanging out with my granddad, watching sports, talking about policy, or discussing the cattle. If my granddad wanted to go somewhere, he liked to have me arrange the security detail. He liked me to bring him his newspapers.

Sometimes he needed help moving from the lounge to the dining table. Small things like that.

I had my own cottage at the back of his property, but I still came home on weekends and dropped in to hang out as often as I could. The Old Man was growing frail. Our relationship came full circle as I stepped in to care for him with the same protective instinct that led him to take me in when I was a kid. I helped arrange outings and visitors. People would call: "Hey, this person is in town and would like to meet your grandfather." He was glad to meet with foreign leaders and dignitaries, and he was fine with most of the celebrities too. He loved Mama Obama and her family and always enjoyed seeing his old friend, Holyfield. In general, he was happy to see people, so when Aunt Zindzi asked if I would facilitate a brief visit she'd arranged for R. Kelly, I said okay.

She told the Old Man about Kelly's philanthropy and efforts to help Africans and African Americans, military families, and children in need. "This is a brilliant musician and a really good guy," she said. "He's in Africa, and he wants to make a side trip over here to meet you and sing something for you."

The Old Man was cool with that. I don't know if he knew about the controversy surrounding the guy, and I didn't want to sabotage my aunt by mentioning it. My granddad said to give the go-ahead to R. Kelly's people, so I did.

On the appointed day, the entourage shows up, and we're all, "Hey, how's it going?" All good. We go to my granddad's lounge, and R. Kelly very respectfully says, "It's an honor to meet you, sir. Thank you for making time to see me, Madiba." And this is where it gets weird. The Old Man just sits there. He does not utter one word. Somebody says something about R. Kelly doing a benefit concert for the Special Olympics in Angola. Nothing. He sits there like Stonehenge.

Meanwhile, R. Kelly wants to sing for Madiba. There's a piano in the lounge area, and it has casters on the bottom, so a couple of security guys go to push it into the middle of the room. My granddad sees this happening and barks, "Hey! What are you doing with my piano?"

I set my hand on his arm. "Granddad, it's okay. Granddad, they're just bringing it a little closer so you can hear better."

He's like, "Hmph. Okay."

So R. Kelly gets on the piano, and it is beautiful, but right in the middle of the song, my granddad reaches over to the side table and gets his newspaper and rattles it open in front of himself. I'm like, *Oh! Damn. That's cold.*

"Granddad, please. Let the man finish."

He noisily folds the paper in his lap. R. Kelly finishes, and everybody claps. He comes over and sits in the chair next to my granddad and thanks Madiba for the visit and for being such an inspiration. Someone takes a photo. Again, the Old Man is sitting there silent as a boulder, so R. Kelly shakes my hand and says, "Hey, man, thanks again. This was amazing."

"Ndaba," says my granddad. He holds up the newspaper and points to a photo of a famous South African rugby player. "Do you know who this is?"

"It's, um . . . it's Bryan Habana, Granddad."

"Good."

He opens the paper and continues his morning routine as I show everyone out.

I didn't know what to say. This was so utterly unlike my grandfather, who was always respectful, humble, generous, and open and had brought me up to be the same way. I went back to the lounge and sat next to him again, thinking, *What just happened?*

I asked, "How are you today, Granddad? Feeling okay?"

"Good. I'm good," he said. "How are you today, Ndaba?"

"I'm . . . wow. I'm okay, Granddad. I think I'll head out though."

I felt bad for R. Kelly. There are few things worse than meeting your hero who turns out to be someone else, but I seriously doubt that there are any heroes who are actually the person they've been built up to be. It's like me idolizing my big brother. My granddad never wanted to be idolized that way. He was consistently humble all his life. He knew that the heroes who fall hardest are the ones who buy into their own PR.

I honestly didn't know what to make of this incident, but I decided not to allow any more visitors to the house. I had already okayed a request from Kanye West, so I had to tell his people, "Kanye's still welcome to come to the house and meet the family, but Madiba won't be able to see him." He didn't flip out, as far as I know, but he had zero interest in meeting any of us if he wasn't getting to meet The Mandela Who Matters. My granddad never made those sort of distinctions. I knew the R. Kelly thing was something else. I thought about it a lot. Why did he point out that photo of Habana?

My interpretation of it hit me a few weeks later. I think he was basically saying, "Look, man, I see all these American artists, and I don't mind meeting them, but do you know who *this* is?" Kweku and I talked a good game about elevating the image of Africa, but I had to admit, the constant strobe light of American celebrity throughout the world is pretty hard to ignore. It's like, "Hey, your beloved South African icon is standing over there, but—wait, *what?* Jay-Z! Get the oxygen masks!" So maybe this was not about R. Kelly at all. Maybe he was telling me to look away from that neon "America!" sign and see the greatness that surrounds me right here in my own country. My granddad was asking me, "Do you know your own African heroes?"

Because the children—the young—we're the ones who don't hear the enchanted song. We're supposed to be close enough to the ground that we still think wealth and fame are illusions. Because they are. And whoever you may be, wherever you may live, if you don't have a South African playlist on your Spotify, you are seriously missing out.

Maybe that's what my granddad was trying to tell me.

Or maybe he was just constipated. Or his socks felt wrong. He had always been very particular. It was a survival mechanism for him when he needed it, and when he no longer needed it, that was what he was used to. Like building the replica of the warden's house in Qunu. He was already an old man when he came out of prison. After Walter Sisulu died, Madiba said, "We watched each other as our backs bent lower and lower over the years." Now he was in his nineties. So he was not likely to change, and having devoted his entire life to the good of others, he'd earned the right to be particular. We were all happy to accommodate him as he maintained his old routine: breakfast, newspapers, a little TV sometimes—boxing or NatGeo—followed by afternoon tea. Every once in a while, there would be a health scare, and the stress of that was magnified by the whole world speculating that he was going to die every time he went into the hospital. It didn't matter if he was being treated for pneumonia or an ingrown toenail; we could count on the reporters storming us every time we walked out the door.

Auntie Maki got cross about it sometimes. "What other president had to put up with this prying into personal details? Nobody! There was never a white president who was so scrutinized."

I could have pointed out to her that there was never a white president so well loved, but when Auntie Maki is cross, it's better to give her a lot of elbow room.

To care for an elder is the greatest honor, and I tried to arrange my life around his needs as much as I could. He kept his outings to a minimum, but nothing could keep him from the hospital when my son Lewanika was born. All the nurses and the doctors were excited to see his great grandfather, but they maintained the calm, quiet atmosphere of the maternity ward. He sat in a chair, holding the baby in his arms, quietly singing an old Xhosa song. I wish I'd asked him to teach it to me. I don't remember it. But it's still there, somewhere in that deep part of Lewanika's spirit, close to where his Legend is stored.

"What should I name him?" I asked.

He said, "Why don't you call him Ngubencuka?" (A Xhosa ancestor's name that means "the wolf's blanket.")

I nodded. "I like that for a middle name. I think his first name should be Lewanika, after my father."

The Old Man smiled. "Good. Lewanika. Very good."

I found it harder to be away from home after that, but there was a lot going on. I became a global ambassador for the Joint United Nations Programme on HIV and AIDS. Kweku and I went to Brazil, to the *favelas*—the hard-hit slums—and talked to orphanage administrators and sex workers, encouraging them to keep up the fight against misinformation and the ravages of HIV/AIDS. We promised to help them break the silence and reclaim a place in society. We looked at ways modern technology could be used to connect needs to the needful, not just those with HIV/AIDS, but also those with malaria and TB and so on. Fighting to raise life expectancy was high on our agenda, but we felt strongly that it was impossible to address this—or any other issue—without addressing the mind-blowing economic disconnect between the small, overwhelmingly white minority who composed 15 percent of the population and controlled 90 percent of the wealth in South Africa.

On a brief stopover at home, I helped my granddad out to the garden, where he could sit in a comfortable chair and get some fresh air. He was quiet, but I was totally taken up with everything I was doing.

"Entrepreneurship is key to the economy, right? And education is key to entrepreneurship. I mean, I just got back from France—beautiful country. Everywhere you look, there's art, architecture. It's great. But I see this gold statue on top of a building, and I go, 'Hmm. Interesting. I don't see a lot of gold mines in France. Do they even have a gold mine?' So I do a little research, and of course, that gold—that particular statue—it came from Africa. From Mali, to be exact. And then I look at Mali, and I see this grinding poverty, and I look at Paris. I don't see any poverty there—or very little."

The Old Man huffed and raised his eyebrows. He'd been fighting a persistent cough.

"I know, I know," I said. "Poverty exists in Paris. I know that, but I don't see any Parisians risking their lives to peddle a little tiny raft across the Mediterranean Sea to Mali, okay? That ain't happening. It's not about poverty; it's about opportunities."

"So what do you mean by all this?" he asked. "What are you saying to them? 'Give me back my gold! Let my people go!'"

"No, I'm not saying, 'Let my people go.' I'm saying, 'Let my people *live*.' Let them be rewarded for their labor. Pay them fairly for their natural resources. Don't give three euro to a charity to help them. Help them by investing in African business. Help them build processing plants and universities and infrastructure."

This wasn't my last conversation with my grandfather. In some ways, I wish it had been. He still loved tackling these big ideas and issues, and he was gratified to see me and Kweku stepping up to take them on.

In December 2013, Kweku and I were in Brazil to participate in events leading up to the World Cup, powering through a tight schedule of media and appearances. Auntie Maki called and said, "Madiba is very ill, Ndaba. You and Kweku should come home."

"Um...okay. Yeah. We'll cut it short, but we have to do this thing tomorrow, Auntie Maki. We can't bail on it. We'll head home right after."

After I hung up, I said to Kweku, "That's just Auntie Maki. She's always calling us to come home when Madiba is sick, and every time, we go home, and he's fine." We agreed that we should leave after the last event, the FIFA World Cup draw.

He was a mighty cedar tree in my mind. My invincible granddad. The idea that I would never see him again—that was unthinkable. So I didn't think that. Instead I thought about everything we had to do the next day. But the next day, Auntie Maki called again. She spoke with Kweku first. He said nothing. Just handed the phone to me. And I said nothing. Just listened.

"He's gone," she said.

The words hit the back of my knees like an axe. I had to tell myself to blink. To breathe. Strength and stoicism are two qualities that were carved into my character from the time I was a little boy. I knew, because I'd already lost both my parents, that this initial throat punch would pass, and then a wave of grief would hit me, and it would last for a long time. I cried a lot that day. I have never cried like that before or since. My brother Kweku held me, and after ten minutes or so, I went in the bathroom to dip cold water on my face. We made a few calls, arranged flights, and made the two-hour drive back to our hotel. The car was silent.

Ndaba.

Yes, Granddad?

I'm thinking of going to the Eastern Cape to spend the rest of my days. Are you going to come with me?

Yes, of course.

Good. Good.

I went with him to the Eastern Cape. My family and I. We drove for what seemed like an eternity, through rolling hills and across expansive savannahs to the place that was once called the Transkei. The colonial government had set aside this "homeland" (which could better be described as "reservation," but only because it was too unwieldy to be called "concentration camp") where they could warehouse black people while the government debased them, robbed them, tore apart their families, and cut them off from the rest of the world.

And then Nelson Mandela happened.

Akukho rhamncwa elingagqumiyo emngxumeni walo.

"There is no beast that does not roar in its own den."

You alone reign over your own spirit. No weight, no spear, no oppressor can take that self-sovereignty from you. While my grandfather was at Robben Island, he wrote to the Commissioner of Prisons, "I have never regarded any man as my superior either in my life outside or inside prison."

Your resolve—your truth—that is the voice that roars within you. My grandfather taught me to listen to that voice within myself.

Ubuntu

Afterword

The world mourned Madiba's passing. Every media outlet was swamped with eulogies and tributes. Everywhere I went, I heard the resonant sound of his voice on TV and radio and internet. Dignitaries, world leaders, American presidents, and celebrities crowded the stands at his funeral in Qunu, and tens of thousands crowded into a memorial service at the football stadium in Soweto. I stood before the gathering in Qunu and read out the story of my grandfather's life.

"It is with deep sadness that the government and the world has learnt of the passing of the father of South Africa's democracy, Nelson Rolihlahla Mandela. He passed on peacefully in the company of his family around 20:50 on the 5th of December 2013. The man who became one of the world's greatest icons was born in Mvezo, Transkei, on 18 July 1918, to Noqaphi Nosekeni and Gadla Henry Mandela. His father was the key counselor and advisor to the Thembu royal house. After his father's death in 1927, the young Rolihlahla became the ward of Chief Jongintaba Dalindyebo and the acting regent of the Thembu nation.

"It was at the Thembu royal homestead that his personality, values, and political views were shaped. There can be no doubt that the young man went on to bring about some of the most significant and remarkable changes in South African history and politics. It is through Mandela that the world cast its eyes on South Africa and took notice of the severe and organized repression of black South Africans. Yet, it was also through Mandela that the world would learn the spirit of endurance, the triumph of forgiveness, and the beauty of reconciliation. Indeed, the story of Nelson Mandela is so much so the story of South Africa.

"When he was only 25 years old, Nelson Mandela joined the African National Congress. His political career would span decades more, as he himself said: 'The struggle is my life.' The young Mandela also qualified and practiced as a lawyer. Together with Oliver Tambo, he opened the first black legal practice in Johannesburg.

"In the 1940s, he was instrumental in the formation of the radical ANC Youth League, which was determined to change the face of politics. Mandela was elected the League's National Secretary in 1948 and President in 1952. Much of the years that followed saw Mandela deeply involved in activism, rallying for political change against the increasingly aggressive apartheid government. He was a key player in the ANC's Campaign for the Defiance of Unjust Laws in 1952 and the Treason Trial in 1961. During this time, he was incarcerated several times under the apartheid laws and banned from political activity. Realizing that the ANC needed to prepare for more intensive struggle, he became an instrumental force behind the formation of a new section of the liberation movement, Umkhonto we Sizwe (MK), as an armed nucleus with a view to preparing for an armed struggle. Mandela was the first commander-in-chief of MK.

"He left the country in 1962 and traveled abroad to arrange guerilla training for members of MK. On his return to South Africa, he was arrested for illegally exiting the country and incitement to strike. Mandela decided to represent himself in court. While on trial, Mandela was charged with sabotage in the Rivonia Trial. This is his famous statement from the dock made in 1964: 'I have fought against white domination, and I have fought against black domination. I have cherished the ideal of a democratic and free society in which all persons live together in harmony and with equal opportunities. It is an ideal which I hope to live for and to achieve. But if needs be, it is an ideal for which I am prepared to die.'

"In the same year Mandela and the other accused were sentenced to life imprisonment in the Rivonia Trial and sent to Robben Island, near Cape Town. While in prison, Mandela rejected the offers made by his jailers to be released on condition that he renounce violence. 'Prisoners cannot enter into contracts,' he said. 'Only free men can negotiate.' He served a total of 27 years in prison for his conviction to fight apartheid and its injustices. Released on 11 February 1990, Mandela plunged wholeheartedly into his life's work, striving to attain the goals he and others had set out almost four decades earlier. In 1991, at the first national conference of the ANC held in South Africa after being banned for decades, Nelson Mandela was elected President of the ANC while his lifelong friend and colleague, Oliver Tambo, became the organization's National Chairperson.

"In a life that symbolizes the triumph of the human spirit, Nelson Mandela accepted the 1993 Nobel Peace Prize, along with F. W. de Klerk, on behalf of all South Africans who suffered and sacrificed so much to bring peace to our land. The era of apartheid formally came to an end on April 27, 1994, when Nelson Mandela voted for the first time in his life, along with his people. However, long before that date it had become clear, even before the start of negotiations at the World Trade Centre in Kempton Park, that the ANC was increasingly charting the future of South Africa.

"Nelson Rolihlahla Mandela was inaugurated as president of a democratic South Africa on 10 May 1994. This world icon worked tirelessly even after the achievement of democracy in South Africa to continue improving lives. Even as he retired from politics, his attention shifted to social issues such as HIV and AIDS and the well-being of the nation's children. As a testimony to his sharp political intellect, wisdom, and unrelenting commitment to make the world a better place, Mandela formed the prestigious group called The Elders, an independent group of eminent global leaders who offer their collective influence and experience to support peace building, help address major causes of human suffering, and promote the shared interests of humanity.

"Mr. Mandela is survived by his wife Graça, three daughters, eighteen grandchildren, and twelve great-grandchildren."

Grateful to have gotten to the end, I folded the paper in my hands, took in a deep breath and shouted, *"Amandla!"*

The power.

And my family responded, *"Ngawethu!"*

It is ours.

IN 2006, LAILA ALI, the daughter of Muhammad Ali, came to visit, and when the Old Man shook her hands, he said, "I was a fighter." Truer words were never spoken. He was a badass when he needed to be, but he was smart when he went into jail and wise when he came out. I didn't always see the difference, but I do now, and I hope I get there someday.

I still live in our house in Houghton. It's a lot to manage on my own, but I manage it with a little help from Andile and Aunt Maki. Every day I wish that Mama Xoli was here, but she's home with her own family now, which is where she wants to be. She certainly earned that. For so many years, her sister took care of her children while

Mama Xoli took care of my granddad and me and our family.

The Old Man's office is still exactly as it was, but all around it, life goes on. On weekends, when my children are with me, they run around and play, and I know that if my grandfather's spirit is lingering here, he's enjoying the sound of their laughter. Our family has struggled since we lost our patriarch, but struggle is not new to this family. The Mandelas are strong. The Mandelas are resilient. The Mandelas endure.

People in my family, like most South Africans, are very social. We're very communal. I hardly do anything by myself. I would never have lunch by myself. Even though it's a normal thing to do, people would be like, "Oh, Ndaba, is everything ok? Are you fine? Why are you alone?" No one goes out to eat by themselves. It's our culture, man, and I love that. I'm comfortable any-where in the world if I have great company. I'm about the people. It's not just a cliché for me; it's the people who make the place. Africans love a good party, a nice birthday, a family holiday dinner. At this writing, we're making plans to celebrate Madiba's one-hundredth birthday, and it's going to be literally a "party all over the world."

I believe in *Ubuntu*, the essential interdependence of humankind. This idea was fostered by my grandfather in

my formative years and resonates in my gut as an unde-
niable truth because I see it in action all around me on a
regular basis. I believe positive changes will come to our
world, but I know that those changes will come only in
concert with unity, understanding, and action.

"When a traveler comes to your village," said Madiba,
"if he doesn't have to ask for food and water, that is
Ubuntu." It's not just that you share what you have;
it's that you anticipate the needs of another and you've
already made sure your own house is in order so you are
in a position to care for others. A better way of addressing yourself is the first step to lifting up the community
around you. You empower yourself, and then you reach
out to others.

We live in one world, and it is all interconnected, but
we need to make sure that we understand how we are
treating each other. We must strive for a more prosperous world for all. We must work to close the gap that
exists between rich and poor, recognizing our common
humanity. We can't fight terrorism with terrorism; we
can win that battle only with unity. Clearly, our governments will never do that for us. We have to change the
world, starting within our own hearts and working outward. We must take control of our own destiny and not
leave it in the hands of those who think they have all the
power. They don't. I am living proof, because I was born

into apartheid, and now I'm free. They didn't take those shackles off me voluntarily. Someone had to stand up for me. Someone had to be a fighter.

What would happen if you stood up right now—on the bus, on an airplane, in the library, on the school playground, all alone in your room? Just stand up right now and hold your hand out toward the future and speak this truth to that person you will be tomorrow:

> *It is in our hands.*
> *It IS in our hands.*
> *To change the world.*
> *Together, we can achieve everything.*

Okay. Now you can sit down again. How did it go? Did someone smile in your direction? Did you start a conversation or perhaps plant a seed in their mind about what's possible for them?

I've been presented with an extraordinary lifetime of opportunities to reach people with a message that combines new ideas with my grandfather's legacy of peace, hope, and positive change. I'm constantly traveling to different parts of the world, speaking to a growing audience of young people who hunger for change and inspiration. As social media and Internet access expand around the globe, Madiba's timeless message promises to resonate for generations to come. I hope to see you out there sometime. I appreciate your taking the time to read this book.

As a mentor and a father, I share with my grandfather a profound sense of humble gratitude, hope, and responsibility. I wish the Old Man could see Lewanika now—seven years old, starting to read, and always quick to stand up for his little sister. Not that anyone needs to stand up for her. At the age of four, she is so feisty and fierce. I love it. I see in my children all that blossoming potential my parents and grandparents saw in me. I'll continue to do my best to be the person they hoped I would be, setting before my son the same example that was set before me, lifting him up, knowing that one day he'll go to the mountain and return to me a man.

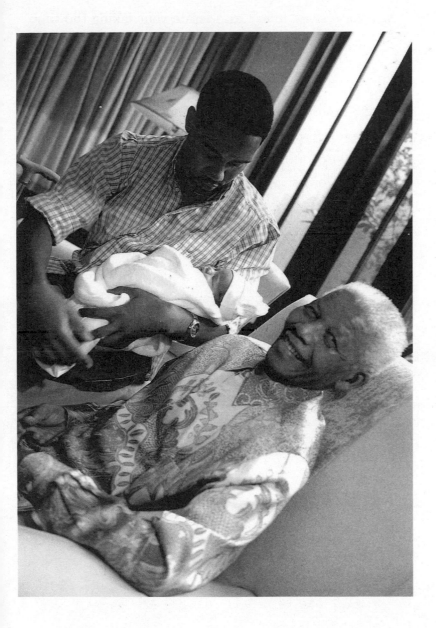

Acknowledgments

This is my truth as I remember it. Dialogue has been reconstructed for dramatic purposes, using letters, videos, and public records. I've done my best to stay true to the spirit of conversations, events, and relationships portrayed in this book based on my unique perspective. Others may remember it differently, based on their unique perspective, and I respect that. My journey has taught me a great deal about history, politics, and economics, and in this book, I share my opinion and respect the differing opinions of others. While I've spoken candidly here about my use of marijuana, I do not condone underage drinking, use of marijuana, or any kind of substance abuse in general. No part of this manuscript should be construed or misconstrued as medical or legal information, testimony or advice. My opinions do not necessarily reflect the opinions of Africa Rising, UNAIDS, the Mandela family, or any organizations who have employed me or hosted me as a speaker or any organizations who may employ or host me in the future. Thanks to my agent Albert Lee and his team at Aevitas Creative, my editor Michelle Howry and her team at Hachette, my collaborator Joni Rodgers and her agent Cindi Davis-Andress.

I thank God Almighty for allowing me to be able to work on this project over the past two years and having it come to fruition. I thank the Lord Almighty for giving me the best gift all, my greatest inspiration and motivation, my two beautiful children. Daddy is not perfect. I've made mistakes and disappointed you—probably not for the last time. Please, know that no matter what, your father loves you more than anything in this world. I'd like to thank Khomotso, the mother of my kids, for being a good mom and taking care of my precious little ones.

ACKNOWLEDGMENTS

Thank you, Andile, for being there and just being a good, good brother, no matter what. Mbuso, I hope you read this book. I'm still your brother, no matter what. Let's just respect each other. After all, it's all we got. Mandla, no man is an Island. Our grandfather talked about forgiveness. There's a lesson we can all learn from him and his life. Let's share and continue this great legacy we have inherited.

Aunt Maki, thank you for being there for me. Do not tire; it's a long road ahead. Love you, Mama Bear. Tukwini, my sister, where would I be without you and your protection? I know you've always got my back. Kweku, my brother, you already know, boy, we started this shit, we gonna continue this shit till the wheels come rolling off, and that means for life, my brother. Gada Gada, up and down we go, but together we shall go farther than we can ever imagine. If Grandma Winnie's passing has taught us anything, it's that we are male heads of this family. Remember what she told us about the apartheid museum? She was not only talking about that, but the country in general, my brother. To the rest of my family: I love all of you. We don't always see eye to eye, but please, let's support each other as much as we can. Slege Mistro the God, Dice Makgothi: Don't be afraid of your destiny. You are more powerful than you think.

ACKNOWLEDGMENTS

You know I'll do anything in my power to make sure you get there, and I believe you're there for me to be able to reach that as well.

To my fellow South Africans: We have come a long way, but the struggle is not yet over. Now we fight for economic emancipation. Land is very much part of that rebuilding, but it goes hand in hand with equipping ourselves with the necessary skills. Owning the land alone will not turn the tide of this divided country and economy we have inherited. African brothers and sisters without unity and reigniting that solidarity, we shall never achieve our destiny, creating the independent, united, prosperous continent we know it ought to be. We are our own worst enemy. Divided we fall. Together we stand. To those in the greater diaspora: We need you like we need each other. Learn about your roots. Travel to your origin. Smile every time you see a fellow African. You never know where that might lead us. Greatness lies within all of us. That's what Nelson Mandela taught me. Let us take our rightful place in this earth and remind the people of the world of our common humanity, the one destiny we share as human beings. Let go of your prejudice. This world does not revolve around you. Humanity cannot continue repeating the same mistakes. It is time we move forward as one people, and that can only be achieved if we work together as one.

Ndaba Mandela
Johannesburg, South Africa
2018

About the Author

Author/activist Ndaba Thembekile Zweliyajika Mandela is an outspoken influencer and change agent on the African continent and in the arena of international politics. He was born in South Africa in 1982 as his grandfather, Nelson Mandela, endured a third decade in prison on Robben Island. Ndaba spent his early childhood in the Transkei, Durban, and Johannesburg, surrounded by a vibrant extended family that included legendary African National Congress activists. Witnessing both the shocking abuses of apartheid and the complex struggle to end it, Ndaba was exposed early to radical ideals of democracy and resistance and developed a keen sense of political awareness beyond the tear gas and police raids on his neighborhood in Soweto.

In 1989, Ndaba met his grandfather for the first time at Victor Verster Prison. A few months later, Nelson Mandela was a free man, and in 1993, shortly before he was elected the first black president of a democratic South Africa, Mandela brought Ndaba to live with him, relishing the opportunity to be there for his grandchildren in a way he was not allowed to be there for his sons and daughters. Being raised by a legend had its challenges, but Ndaba navigated a rocky adolescence and majored in Political Science and International Relations at the University of Pretoria. He graduated in 2009 and began his career as a senior political consultant to the Embassy of Japan in South Africa and client liaison officer for an international asset management group.

Ndaba and his cousin Kweku Mandela are cofounders of Africa Rising, a nonprofit foundation dedicated to the shifting socioeconomic challenges faced by Africans of every color, creed, sexual orientation, and political persuasion. In its first ten years, Africa Rising launched projects and media campaigns taking on AIDS, youth unemployment, education, and other critical issues. One goal for the next ten years is to "build 100 Mandelas" through a leadership program designed around the principles and proactive strategies embodied by Nelson Mandela. Recently named one of BET's "28 Men of Change," Ndaba is passionate about developing Africa as a continent and nurturing a new breed of empowered young Africans throughout the world. He travels widely, speaking about progress, unity, and the Mandela Legacy. He spends his downtime hanging out with friends, keeping up with family, and raising his children with the same core belief his grandfather instilled in him: "Together, as one, we can accomplish anything."